ITALIAN DRAWINGS
AT THE ART INSTITUTE

Recent Acquisitions and Discoveries

The
Art Institute
of Chicago

MUSEUM STUDIES

VOLUME 17, NO. 1

The Art Institute of Chicago
MUSEUM STUDIES

VOLUME 17, NO. 1

Foreword

This issue of *Museum Studies* is devoted to a particular strength in the collections of The Art Institute of Chicago: Italian works on paper of the fifteenth to the eighteenth century. Our intention is not only to highlight the continuing acquisition of Italian drawings in the past ten years, but also to share with the public our growing knowledge of the collection. We present the following articles — on master drawings by Pontormo, Federico Barocci, Rosalba Carriera, and Gian Francesco de' Maineri, and a remarkable monotype by Giovanni Benedetto Castiglione — as part of the museum's continuing effort to catalogue and publish all of its significant Italian drawings and prints.

This effort began, in its latest phase, with the 1979 exhibition and catalogue *Italian Drawings in The Art Institute of Chicago*, organized by Harold Joachim and Suzanne Folds McCullagh; and it has continued with the current Drawings Documentation project, which involves the recataloguing of the entire drawing collection of over 11,000 works and eventually the publication of a comprehensive catalogue encompassing over 2,200 Italian drawings, the first in a series on the department's holdings.

Among the most significant recent acquisitions of the Art Institute is a masterpiece of fifteenth-century Italian drawing, Gian Francesco de' Maineri's *Sacrificial Scene*. A painter who spent much of his time in Ferrara, Maineri was a follower of the well-known Ferrarese artist Ercole de' Roberti. Indeed, the high quality of the Art Institute's *Sacrificial Scene* led many past scholars to attribute the drawing to Roberti. But, as Kristen Lippincott of the Warburg Institute explains in our first essay, a comparison of the styles of fifteenth-century Ferrarese artists shows that the drawing is the work of Maineri. Lippincott examines the religious symbolism of Maineri's *Sacrificial Scene*, and provides a fascinating analysis of the likely purpose of the drawing.

Laura M. Giles, Research Curator for Italian drawings at the Art Institute, has contributed an essay on a major composition study by Pontormo, which she identifies for the first time as a depiction of *Christ before Pilate*. This intricate composition study — with its intense passages of overdrawing and stumping — gives us a vivid sense of the artist's working method, and presents a number of interpretive challenges. Giles examines the puzzling iconographic and stylistic elements of the drawing, and discusses Pontormo's important ties to the work of Albrecht Dürer, Andrea del Sarto, and other artists. An accompanying essay by Harriet K. Stratis, Andrew W. Mellon Fellow in Paper Conservation at the Art Institute, examines closely the paper and media of *Christ before Pilate* and provides a compelling technical analysis of the ambiguities of Pontormo's drawing.

A remarkable story surrounds Barocci's *Christ Child*, the subject of our next essay. As part of our effort to catalogue all of the Art Institute's drawings, I sifted through almost 2,000 previously uncatalogued drawings donated to the museum in 1944 by Katharine Eberley Gurley. Among the works in the Gurley Collection was a striking chalk and pastel drawing of a child that, with its energetic style and its subtle touches of pastel, seemed to me to bear the hand of the mid-sixteenth-century Italian master Federico Barocci. Further research indeed revealed that the *Christ Child* is a study for one of Barocci's early altarpieces known as the *Madonna di San Giovanni*.

One of the masterpieces of the monotype medium is Giovanni Benedetto Castiglione's *God Creating Adam*, which is the subject of Sue Welsh Reed's essay. Commonly believed to have been the inventor of the monotype, Castiglione could achieve marvelous effects simply with an inked plate and a stick, as can be seen in *God Creating Adam*. Reed, an associate curator at the Museum of Fine Arts, Boston, provides a rich and lucid analysis of the religious and artistic sources for *God Creating Adam*, drawing connections between Castiglione and other artists such as Parmigianino and Michelangelo.

Our final essay examines the work reproduced on our cover: Rosalba Carriera's pastel *Young Lady with a Parrot*. Celebrated during her lifetime as the most important woman artist of her period, Rosalba was instrumental in pioneering and refining the art of the pastel portrait. Bernardina Sani of the Università di Siena, a noted expert on Rosalba, places the *Young Lady with a Parrot* within the historical development of the pastel medium, and probes the meaning of Rosalba's mysterious juxtaposition of the parrot and the unknown young lady. We are delighted to close this issue of *Museum Studies* with Rosalba's sensual and provocative pastel.

SUZANNE FOLDS McCULLAGH
Curator of Earlier Prints and Drawings

A Masterpiece of Renaissance Drawing:
A *Sacrificial Scene* by Gian Francesco de' Maineri

KRISTEN LIPPINCOTT

The Warburg Institute, University of London

In 1989, The Art Institute of Chicago acquired one of the great master-pieces of Ferrarese drawing (pl. 2 and fig. 1). Beautifully constructed and finely drawn, the *Sacrificial Scene* is an outstanding example of late fifteenth-century craftsmanship and a fascinating cultural and historical document. It tells us a great deal about Ferrarese art, fifteenth-century draw-ing practices, religious iconography, and early Renaissance attitudes toward the past.

Executed in black ink and wash, with highlights added in lead white, the drawing is an imaginative reconstruction of an ancient sacrifice. Two priests, one wearing a turban and the other bald, attend the sacrificial fire. The turbaned priest stirs the ashes of the fire with a long stick, in anticipation of the sacrificial victim's blood being poured onto its flames. The other priest holds a turban in his left hand and a small, covered dish (probably for scented oils) and a censer in his right. Standing atop the altar is a small statuette of a nude female—presumably the deity to whom the offering is being made—whose private parts are modestly covered by a long swath of drapery. She carries a spearlike arrow in her upraised right hand, suggesting that she may represent either Diana in her guise as the moon goddess, Luna, or *Venus victrix*. In the foreground of the composition, another turbaned priest slits the throat of a small animal whose exact species, while hard to determine, seems closest in shape to a fawn or new-born calf. The third priest is attended by a youth who holds forth a large, flat dish, or *patera*, to catch the blood that will soon flow from the animal's wounds.

As grisly as all this may seem, the drawing is actually serene and elegant. The scene is presented as a religious event—meditative, slow-moving, balanced, and harmonious. Much of this mood is created by the drawing's artful composition. The artist utilized all his skills in combining a number of features whose overall effect is reassuring to the viewer. The classically inspired architecture establishes a tone of refined grace. Although heavily corniced, the architecture is neither fussy nor distractingly decorative. It is clean, simple, and straightforward. The figures, in turn, are arranged nearly symmetrically around the altar, balancing the right and left halves of the drawing. Furthermore, their four heads outline an arc that complements the

FIGURE 1. Gian Francesco de' Maineri (Italian, active 1489–1506). *Sacrificial Scene* (detail of pl. 2), 1488/90. Pen and black ink, with brush and gray and brown wash, heightened with lead white (partially discolored), on cream laid paper; 41.8 x 30 cm. The Art Institute of Chicago, Regenstein Collection (1989.686). Impressive for its high quality and large dimensions, this drawing is intriguing on many levels: the history of its attribution, its possible purpose and meaning, and how it reveals Renaissance interpretations of the past.

7

major architectural feature of the setting, the curved niche within which the sacrificial altar is set. The drawing is bisected vertically by the central altar and its goddess, and horizontally at the level of the altar table. Added to this very solid compositional structure, the even depiction of light and shade contributes to the drawing's overall sense of tranquility. The drapery of the figures' robes, although complex, lacks the excited, static charge typical of mid-fifteenth-century Ferrarese painting and drawing.

Late Fifteenth-Century Ferrarese Painting and Misunderstandings about Ercole de' Roberti

For most of its documented history, this remarkable drawing has been attributed to the Ferrarese artist Ercole de' Roberti, who served as court painter to the Este, the ruling ducal family of Ferrara, from the late 1480s until his death, in 1496.[1] The reasoning behind this attribution in many ways reveals less about the *Sacrificial Scene* than about the development of art-historical approaches to Ferrarese art.

During the Renaissance, Ferrara was one of the major city-states of the Italian peninsula. Its income was largely derived from the trade and commerce that had developed due to its fortuitous position on the banks of the Po River, the great east-west trade route of northern Italy. Records suggest that Ferrara had more square feet of frescoed and decorated walls than any other city in Italy. Sadly, however, when the Este family fell from power, in the last years of the sixteenth century, Ferrara was virtually destroyed by a successive series of invading armies. Very little survives of the glory that was Renaissance Ferrara. Scholars have been left with the difficult task of trying to re-create a lost ambience from the few fragments and documents that remain.

For the past century, art historians have tended toward a peculiar sort of oversimplification when it came to the attribution of works of art that were thought to be connected, in some way, with Ferrara. Since only a handful of artists' names had been discovered in the documents, all extant Ferrarese paintings and drawings were divided among these few names. The "better" pieces were attributed to whoever was known to be the court artist during the period to which the painting was assigned; the mediocre pieces were handed over to followers or to fictitious, art-historical creations such as the Italian connoisseur Roberto Longhi's invention: "Vicino da Ferrara" (literally, "close to [the style of someone] from Ferrara"). The former attribution of the Art Institute's drawing to Roberti, therefore, is not particularly informative, since virtually every late fifteenth-century work from Ferrara of this quality has been assigned to him at one time or another.

Only recently have art historians begun to acknowledge the frustrating complexities of Ferrarese art. Much of this has to do with understanding the role of the court artist in a north Italian duchy. Officially, he seems to have been personally responsible for every decorated object in the ducal territory. This task involved composing great fresco cycles; subcontracting and supervising the teams of painters involved in these great undertakings; repairing damaged works of art; painting theater sets, marriage chests, heraldic banners, and horse-trappings (such as bridles and saddles); constructing and decorating the odd bit of furniture; painting illusionistic scenery for summer parties, and so on. In a sense, the role of a court artist in the fifteenth century was not unlike that of a leading Hollywood movie producer in the 1930s and 1940s, except that the artist was consistently a "hands-on" member of the team. The court painter set the "visual style" for the court and, to a greater or lesser degree, everyone who worked under him painted in this style as long as it remained fashionable. Only careful study reveals the individual personalities of the different artists active in Ferrara during the latter years of the fifteenth century. Consequently, the oeuvres of artists known to have worked closely with Roberti or his immediate followers, such as Panetti, Mazzolino, Coltellini, Grimaldi, the young Costa, and Maineri—to whom the museum's drawing is presently attributed—have only begun to be explored. Indeed, the history behind the present attribution of the Art Institute's *Sacrificial Scene* to Gian Francesco de' Maineri is a case in point. Understanding why the drawing might be attributable to Maineri rests on appreciating the sort of detective work that goes into any study of fifteenth-century Ferrarese art.

The Peculiar History of the *Pala Strozzi*

The story begins with a large altarpiece, the *Enthroned Madonna and Child with Saints William and John the Baptist*, in the National Gallery, London (fig. 2). This panel is commonly known as the *Pala Strozzi*, since originally it had been commissioned by the Strozzi family for the high altar of the Oratorio della Concezione (known as Santa Maria della Scala) in Ferrara. Since 1880, the *Pala Strozzi* had been attributed to the largely hypothetical persona "Ercole Grandi."[2] In 1934, however, Longhi rejected the attribution of the altarpiece to "Ercole Grandi" on the altogether sensible premise that

FIGURE 2. Lorenzo Costa (Italian, 1460–1535) and Gian Francesco de' Maineri. *Enthroned Madonna and Child with Saints William (of Aquitaine?) and John the Baptist (The Pala Strozzi)*, 1498–99. Oil on panel; 247 x 163.8 cm. London, National Gallery (no. 1119). The Ferrarese artist Maineri was probably responsible for the composition of this altarpiece, which is closely related to the Art Institute's *Sacrificial Scene*.

FIGURE 3. Gian Francesco de' Maineri. *Madonna and Child*, c. 1490. Oil on panel; 48.5 x 35.7 cm. Turin, Galleria dell'Accademia Albertina.

FIGURE 4. Gian Francesco de' Maineri. *Holy Family*, c. 1500. Oil on panel; 60 x 44 cm. Formerly Ferrara, Testa Collection. This panel and the *Madonna and Child* (fig. 3) are two of three extant paintings signed by Maineri. They serve as important touchstones in attributing a body of work to this artist.

such an artist never existed. He argued that the *Pala Strozzi* seemed to be the product of a collaboration of two different artists, one of whom was certainly the Ferrarese painter Lorenzo Costa.[3] Prompted by Longhi's suggestion, the English connoisseur Philip Pouncey decided to have the *Pala Strozzi* x-radiographed. This revealed that the entire panel had been repainted, except for Saint William's armor and left hand. Furthermore, the repainting had been done by someone other than the original artist. Pouncey agreed with Longhi's attribution of the final painting of the altarpiece to Costa, and suggested, by means of comparison to other signed works, that the original painting had been done by the then little-known Ferrarese painter Gian Francesco de' Maineri.[4] Pouncey's role in untangling the history of the *Pala Strozzi* is interesting because he was also responsible for the attribution of the Art Institute's *Sacrificial Scene* to Maineri.[5]

Born in Parma sometime between 1460 and 1470, Gian Francesco de' Maineri is first recorded in Ferrara in 1489 as having received payment for painting some "green batons" (*per fare verde zerti bastoni*) in the garden of the city's great Castello.[6] He seems to have traveled regularly between Ferrara and Mantua. Documents dating from 1489–93, 1502–03, and 1505 place Maineri in Ferrara at these times; and records from 1498–99, 1504, and 1506 show him in Mantua during these periods. Indeed, this constant "to-ing and fro-ing" upset more than one patron who found himself with an unfinished commission on his hands.

This, in fact, seems to be the explanation behind the peculiar history of the *Pala Strozzi*. One series of letters, running through November and December of 1498, records a heated episode between the agents of Isabella d'Este, Ferrarese wife of the Mantuan marquis Francesco II Gonzaga, and the brothers Carlo and Camillo Strozzi. Isabella had called Maineri to Mantua to paint her portrait. In answering the marquise's summons, Maineri apparently abandoned a large altarpiece he had been painting for the Strozzi brothers, which he had promised to finish by Christmas 1498. Understandably upset, the Strozzi retaliated by threatening to sue Maineri's wife, who had remained in Ferrara, for damages and interest. Isabella was furious. She wrote to the Strozzi, loyal patrician subjects of her father, Duke Ercole I d'Este, and told them to leave off bothering about Maineri, as he was now working for her! The Strozzi, given little alternative, gracefully bowed out.[7] Pouncey suggested that Costa's single trip to Ferrara in 1499 (his only return visit to his hometown after he had left it in 1485) coincides perfectly with the probable date for his completion of the *Pala Strozzi*.[8] The most plausible scenario, then, is that Costa was called to Ferrara by the Strozzi expressly to finish the huge altarpiece that Maineri had left incomplete—hence, Maineri's underpainting, visible only by means of X-radiography, underneath the final surface of what is essentially Costa's painting.

The Paintings of Gian Francesco de' Maineri

Our knowledge of Maineri's work rests on three signed paintings: a *Madonna and Child* in the Galleria dell'Accademia Albertina, Turin (fig. 3); a similar, but probably slightly later, *Holy Family*, formerly in the Testa

FIGURE 5. Anonymous painter (Italian). *Madonna and Child*, 1500/1505. Tempera or oil on panel; 52 x 35 cm. The Art Institute of Chicago, Charles H. and Mary F. S. Worcester Collection (1947.90). This painting, produced by someone in the circle of the Ferrarese painter Ercole de' Roberti, exhibits a sweetness of style that was pervasive throughout Italy in the late fifteenth century.

Collection, Ferrara (fig. 4), and a *Head of Saint John the Baptist* in the Pinacoteca di Brera, Milan.[9] Furthermore, at least seven partial copies of Maineri's *Holy Family* and a similar number of his *Christ Carrying the Cross* have been uncovered to date. Such a quantity of nearly identical paintings suggests that there must have been a tremendous market for small, devotional paintings in and around Ferrara and Mantua, for which Maineri was a leading supplier.[10]

The small nucleus of secure works already tells us a great deal about Maineri's painting style. As one might expect, he was strongly influenced by Ercole de' Roberti, an influence that Maineri never wholly outgrew. Even in his mature works, the solidity of form, monumentality of the figures, and overall color schemes hark back to Roberti's painting style of the late 1480s and 1490s. At the very least, this debt could be attributed to the fact that Roberti's tenure as court painter in Ferrara overlapped with Maineri's early years in the town. It does seem, however, that the link between the two artists may have been closer: Maineri may even have been trained in Roberti's shop.

One incident supports such a thesis: among all the artists available in Ferrara, it was Maineri who was hired to finish an important commission that had been left incomplete at Roberti's death in 1496.[11] Furthermore, stylistic examination of one painting, the *Gravaghi Madonna and Child*, formerly in the Canto Collection, Milan, seems to indicate that Maineri was

FIGURE 6. Ercole de' Roberti. *Enthroned Madonna and Child with Saints Elizabeth, Anne, Augustine and the Beatified Pietro degli Onesti (The Pala Portuense)*, c. 1480–81. Oil on panel; 323 x 240 cm. Milan, Pinacoteca di Brera. Many stylistic and compositional features of this altarpiece by Roberti, such as its rigidly geometrical composition, the shapes of the heads, and the arrangement of the drapery folds, can be found in the work of Maineri.

FIGURE 7. Ercole de' Roberti. *Saint Jerome*, c. 1480. Oil on panel; 35.2 x 23.5 cm. London, Barlow Collection.

called upon to finish the Christ Child and the hands of the Madonna in a composition that otherwise seems to be by Roberti.[12] Indeed, Longhi made a similar suggestion regarding a *Madonna and Child* in the Art Institute (fig. 5), which recalls Roberti's work in both its composition and form. The finish, however, is slightly more elegant and langorous than is usual in Roberti's autograph works and the details are slightly too precious. Longhi, no great fan of Maineri's, characterized the painting as showing Ercole "replaced... by his more decadent and affected [literally, 'strained'] pupil."[13]

Such full-scale condemnation seems unwarranted. Certainly, Maineri was a more refined stylist than Roberti was. But this tendency toward prettiness should not be seen as a defect; instead, it reflects a general trend toward what is often termed "the sweet style" seen in the work of artists active during the last decades of the fifteenth century and evident in the paintings of such Emilian artists as Costa and Francia, as well as in the art of the Venetian Giovanni Bellini and of the Umbrian Perugino, not to mention that of the young Raphael Santi. The reason behind this perceptible shift in taste is not clear. Some scholars have suggested that it reflects the deep religious fervor that spread over the Italian peninsula during these years, exemplified by the pervasive influence of the preachings of Girolamo Savonarola. Perhaps it was a reaction to the seemingly interminable wars between the Italian city-states and their neighbors during the latter years of the fifteenth century, evidence of a cultural fatigue and a pervasive desire for retreat from worldy concerns. Perhaps this style was consciously developed as yet another commodity for wealthy aristocratic patrons who wanted something "pretty" to touch and look at. This change in sensibility probably reflects a combination of factors that have yet to be satisfactorily analyzed. Nonetheless, it is into this milieu that one must place Maineri's *Sacrificial Scene*.

Maineri and the Art Institute's *Sacrificial Scene*

The Chicago drawing fits most comfortably into Maineri's early career, when he was still very close to Roberti's style of the 1480s, as exemplified by the latter's *Pala Portuense* in the Brera (fig. 6), the Barlow Collection's *Saint Jerome* (fig. 7), or the now destroyed painting on which Ercole collaborated with his teacher, Francesco del Cossa, the *Pala di San Lazzaro*, formerly in the Staatliche Museen, Berlin (fig. 8). All these works share a self-conscious, geometricizing attitude toward composition. The diagonal posture of the Barlow Collection *Saint Jerome*, for example, actually forms one side of an inverted triangle, which locks the overall structure of the painting into place much in the same way that the V-shaped arc of the priests' heads stabilizes the composition of the *Sacrificial Scene*. The bald head of the priest in the upper right of the drawing also has Robertian precedence (the aforementioned *Saint Jerome*, the same saint in the *Pala di San Lazzaro*, and the Beatified Pietro degli Onesti in the *Pala Portuense*). The priest in the upper left of the drawing sports a beard not dissimilar in form from those worn by Roberti's Saint Jeromes. The drapery style also recalls Roberti's in the way that the cloth is always bundled around the hip and upper thighs, while the lower limbs are partially defined by some sort of material that alternately clings to and protrudes from the figure to create unusual, shelflike folds. The physiognomy of the two figures at the drawing's right strongly resembles Roberti's early work and reflects the influence of Francesco del Cossa.[14] Yet, for all these similarities, the Art Institute sheet is clearly not by Roberti's hand.

FIGURE 8. Francesco del Cossa (Italian, c. 1436–1478) and Ercole de' Roberti. *Enthroned Madonna and Child with Saints Apollonia, Catherine of Alexandria, Augustine, and Jerome (The Pala di San Lazzaro)*, c. 1475/79. Oil on canvas; 309 x 234 cm. Formerly Berlin, Staatliche Museen (destroyed 1945). Photo: Eberhard Ruhmer, *Francesco del Cossa* (Munich, 1959), pl. xx.

FIGURE 9. Ercole de' Roberti. *Study for "The Betrayal of Christ,"* c. 1482/86. Pen and ink on paper; 15 x 21 cm. Florence, Galleria degli Uffizi (no. 1448E). The mature Roberti tended to use drawing as an expressive medium, exploring the layered emotions generated by a given subject.

Despite the fact that the drawing recalls Roberti's paintings, it does not coincide with what we know about his skill as a draftsman. Roberti tended to use drawing as an expressive medium, a tool with which he explored the portrayal of ideas and emotion. This fundamental difference in approach becomes clear when one compares the *Sacrificial Scene* with one of Roberti's mature drawings, such as the *Study for "The Betrayal of Christ"* in the Galleria degli Uffizi, Florence (fig. 9). The *Sacrificial Scene* is a completely different sort of drawing. There is little evidence of creative furor or of the intense study after live models. Instead, the sheet is carefully constructed, painfully accurate in the rendering of detail, and finished to a very high degree. It is more of a demonstration piece, proving the artist's skill and his ability to control the pen-and-ink medium. In this regard, one might argue, it seems to betray the efforts of a young or slightly insecure artist—by no means untalented, but still slightly anxious to "get everything right."

If one compares the *Sacrificial Scene* to other works attributed to Maineri, the similarities are striking. For example, the decorative grotesque on the front of the altar is nearly identical to the carved design that appears on the altar in the Testa Collection *Holy Family* and in one of the copies of this composition now in the Wernher Collection in Luton Hoo, Bedfordshire, England. The architecture found in the Art Institute drawing is close to that of the base of the Madonna's throne in the *Pala Strozzi*, with large, flat, inset panels surrounded by simple, beveled moldings spaced from the crowning cornice by an elegantly proportioned, unornamented architrave (fig. 10). The physiognomic structure of the two prophets' heads in the decorative roundels on the Madonna's throne is extremely close to that of the priest who is slitting the animal's throat in the Chicago drawing. Indeed, the mysterious, small beast also appears in the background of the Turin *Madonna and Child*. All of these aspects seem to confirm Pouncey's attribution of the Chicago drawing to Maineri. It is probably early, executed while he was still very close to Roberti, perhaps while still in his workshop. Many scholars have since recognized the *Sacrificial Scene* as Maineri's first known work.[15] A likely date for the drawing, then, would be sometime before 1490.

Modello Drawings in Fifteenth-Century Italy

The most impressive single feature of the Art Institute's *Sacrificial Scene* is its size. At 41.8 x 30 cm, or about 16½ x 11¾ inches, it is among the largest fifteenth-century drawings known. Indeed, it seems that fifteenth-century papermakers were unable to produce laid paper much larger than this. The sheet's dimensions and the very high quality of the drawing tempt one to suggest that it was intended as a finished product in itself, a presentation piece offered by the artist to a friend or patron whom he wished to please, such as the numerous drawings Michelangelo made for his friend Tommaso de' Cavalieri[16] or, as has been argued, Andrea Mantegna's *Judith* in the Uffizi (fig. 11).

While an intriguing possibility, the likelihood that the Art Institute *Sacrifice* is a presentation drawing is not great. We know painfully little about fifteenth-century drawing practices—too little, in fact, to do much more than generalize—but it seems that presentation drawings were more a phenomenon of the mature, self-assured artist than of the young trainee. Moreover, such drawings are actually extremely rare in the fifteenth century. Mantegna's *Judith*, for example, is more probably a highly finished *modello*—the perfected template upon which a painting is modeled—than a presentation drawing, because at least three small chiaroscuro paintings, which have been attributed to Mantegna or to his immediate circle, seem to depend directly on the drawing for inspiration: one in the National Gallery of Ireland, Dublin (fig. 12); another in the Museum of Fine Arts, Montreal; and a third, a workshop piece, in the National Gallery of Art, Washington, D.C.[17] This duplication suggests that Mantegna's finished drawings were probably studio aids, things he kept around the shop as ready models from which he or his apprentices could produce "made-to-order" paintings. This attitude toward the production of pictures was also employed by Titian, as his numerous compositions of the *Mary Magdalen*, *Diana and Actaeon*, and *Danaë* attest.[18] And, certainly, Maineri, who no doubt knew Mantegna well

FIGURE 10. Detail of figure 2 showing the base of the Madonna's throne, which is similar in structure to the architecture in the Art Institute's *Sacrificial Scene.*

FIGURE 11. Andrea Mantegna (Italian, 1430/31–1506). *Judith with the Head of Holofernes*, 1491. Pen, brown wash, with some heightening in white lead; 38.8 x 25.8 cm. Florence, Galleria degli Uffizi (no. 404E).

FIGURE 12. Andrea Mantegna. *Judith with the Head of Holofernes*, c. 1500. Tempera on linen, mounted on millboard; 46 x 36 cm. Dublin, National Gallery of Ireland (no. 442). This is one of a group of paintings apparently based directly on Mantegna's own highly finished drawing of *Judith* (fig. 11), which itself may have been a presentation piece for a friend or client or, more likely, was a *modello* that he and his workshop assistants used in creating one or more pictures of the same subject.

and was himself the author of at least seven Holy Family paintings and an equal number of paintings depicting *Christ Carrying the Cross,* must have been aware of the advantages of this method of preserving successful designs.

The rather obscure subject matter of the Art Institute's *Sacrificial Scene,* however, makes it unlikely that it was a *modello* for one of Maineri's "best-sellers." Furthermore, as has been noted, the drawing seems a youthful product. Its conscientious execution suggests instead that it is a *modello* for a specific painting or part of a painting, a sort of trial run or test piece in which Maineri could prove to himself or to his patron that he was capable of completing the task at hand. Fifteenth-century *modelli* of this sort are extremely common. One only need cite, for example, the half-dozen *modelli* executed by Domenico Ghirlandaio for his frescoes in the Cappella Torna-buoni in Santa Maria Novella (figs. 13–14) and for the Cappella Sassetti in Santa Trinita, both in Florence.[19] The shear number of *modelli* surviving from the fifteenth century illustrates the extent to which a final, carefully executed drawing was then often considered a required part of the process of making a painting. It represented the final hurdle the artist had to overcome before he actually picked up his brush.

The Representation of Antiquity in Fifteenth-Century Paintings

For what sort of painting did Maineri's *modello* serve? Ironically, one telling aspect of the drawing's iconography is its non-specific nature. We can tell that it represents a sacrificial scene, possibly made to a pagan goddess, but little more. The turbaned priests are presented as antique figures, and their turbans mark them out as "Eastern," but it is unclear whether they are supposed to be Greek, Persian, Arab, or even Old Testament figures. It is hard to tell whether this anonymity was intended or not.

The fifteenth century was still an age of discovery. Despite much research and thought, few during the early Renaissance had a very clear understanding or image of the past. For most, "antiquity" simply meant "from a previous age." The classical past was known largely through literary sources, such as the writings of Pliny, Livy, or Suetonius. This meant that artists, most of whom had little access to or real appreciation of the great monuments of Rome, were forced to rely on humanist scholars for second-hand scraps of knowledge about the marvels of the past.

Thus, in the re-creation of historical or mythological compositions, imagination is often more evident than archeology. Even conscientiously antiquarian draftsmen, such as Ciriaco d'Ancona or Felice Feliciano, who spent hours painstakingly copying antique inscriptions, relied on their knowledge of contemporary events or current pictorial formulae to create their own "classical" scenes. For example, among the relatively faithful drawings after antique monuments added to the fifteenth-century antiquarian Giovanni Marcanova's manuscript in Modena, there is a series of fantastic interpretations of Caesar's palace and scenes of ancient sacrifice, which, although full of isolated antiquarian detail, remain typically late medieval in their overall effect (see figs. 15–16).[20] This demonstrates one of the great disjunctions of art history, the gap between acquired knowledge and intuitive creative response, and well illustrates the art historian Ernst Gombrich's profound observation that people most often draw what they know, rather than what they see.[21] No doubt, Maineri had a fairly good idea of what an "antique sacrifice" must have looked like. One scholar has even suggested that the drawing is a "free variation of an antique type."[22] But this observation seems to misrepresent the focus or aim of the drawing. In the *Sacrificial Scene*, Maineri created an image that was largely the product of his own imagination, a record of what he believed a sacrificial scene ought to look like. The nationality of the priests and exact historical context of the scene are left unclear precisely because they are superfluous to the particular story Maineri was trying to tell.

"Type" and "Antitype" in Renaissance Art

Accepting that the Art Institute's *Sacrificial Scene* is non-specific in its subject matter helps us identify its probable purpose. One extremely popular iconographic *topos* in Christian art is the "type/antitype." Stemming from the writings of the early Church fathers, such as Saint Augustine and Tertullian, this device set up a number of different episodes in the Old Testament,

FIGURE 13. Domenico Ghirlandaio (Italian, 1449–1494). *Annunciation to Zachariah*, 1485/90. Pen and ink and wash; 25.9 x 37.4 cm. Vienna, Graphische Sammlung Albertina (no. 4860). This drawing served as a *modello* for the fresco scene in figure 14.

FIGURE 14. Domenico Ghirlandaio. *Annunciation to Zachariah*, 1485–90. Fresco. Florence, Santa Maria Novella, Cappella Tornabuoni.

FIGURE 15. Anonymous artist (North Italian, fifteenth century) (Felice Feliciano?). *Caesar's Palace*, c. 1465. Pen and ink on parchment. Modena, Biblioteca Estense, cod. lat. 992 (αL.5.15), fol. 27r.

FIGURE 16. Anonymous artist (North Italian, fifteenth century) (Felice Feliciano?). *Scenes of Classical Sacrifices*, c. 1465. Modena, Biblioteca Estense, cod. lat. 992 (αL.5.15), fol. 38r. Even though the early Renaissance was a period of active rediscovery of the past, antiquity continued to be somewhat freely reinvented by artists such as Maineri and his north Italian contemporaries.

classical history, and pagan myths ("types") as the symbolic counterparts to events described in the New Testament ("antitypes"). For example, God speaking to Moses from the Burning Bush was seen as a "type" for the Annunciation to the Virgin (see fig. 17); the Creation of Eve from the rib of Adam was the "type" for the creation of the Church (*Ecclesia*) from the wound in Christ's side (see fig. 18), and so on. The most recurrent "type" for the Crucifixion of Christ was an Old Testament or pagan sacrifice.

The most convenient format for the presentation of "type" and "antitype" was two separate flanking scenes, seen in numerous copies of the *Mirror of Human Salvation* (the *Speculum humanae salvationis*) or the *Moralized Bible (Bible moralisée)*, for example. With the Renaissance penchant for a single, spatially unified pictorial field, the tradition had to be redressed. The new solution was to depict the "type" as a decorative element—either in a simulated painting or a sculptural relief—in the architecture surrounding or supporting the main subject of the picture. Examples of this solution appear throughout Italy during the fifteenth century: the Milanese Bernardo Luini's *Circumcision*, where the Sacrifice of Isaac appears as a simulated bronze roundel decorating the altar upon which the Christ Child is about to be circumcised; Bellini's *Christ the Redeemer*, which features a classical sacrifice inserted in the marble panels behind the main figure (fig. 19); Mantegna's fresco *The Trial of Saint James the Great*, in the Chiesa degli Eremitani, Padua, where the marble relief of a pagan sacrifice is embedded in the wall of the triumphal arch above James's head; and Ghirlan-

FIGURE 17. Anonymous miniaturist (Italian, fourteenth century). Page from *Speculum humanae salvationis*. Pen and ink on parchment. Paris, Bibliothèque nationale, ms. lat. 9584, chap. 7. Since the early Middle Ages, Christian writers and artists tended to interpret classical myths, ancient history, and the Old Testament as symbolic counterparts ("types") to episodes in the New Testament ("antitypes"). Here *Moses and the Burning Bush* is coupled with the *Annunciation to the Virgin*.

FIGURE 18. Anonymous miniaturist (French, mid-thirteenth century). Page from *Bible moralisée*. Vienna, Oesterreichisches National-bibliothek, cod. 2554, fol. 1v. Photo: facsimile edition (Graz and Paris, 1973). Here the *Creation of Eve from Adam's Rib* is the "type" and the *Creation of the Church from the Wound in Christ's Side* the "antitype."

FIGURE 19. Giovanni Bellini (Italian, c. 1430–1516). *Christ the Redeemer*, c. 1465. Tempera on panel; 47 x 34 cm. London, National Gallery (no. 1233). Renaissance artists preferred scenes unified both in terms of time and space; their symbolic pairings of "type" and "antitype" was often achieved by including the "type" as a decorative feature in the "antitype" scene. Here a pagan sacrifice serves as the "type" for Christ's sacrifice.

FIGURE 20. Lorenzo Costa. *Enthroned Madonna and Child with Members of the Family of Giovanni II Bentivoglio (Madonna dei Bentivoglio)*, 1488. Fresco. Bologna, San Giacomo Maggiore, Cappella dei Bentivoglio.

FIGURE 21. Lorenzo Costa. Detail of figure 21 showing sacrificial scene at the base of the Madonna's throne. Most likely, Maineri's *Sacrificial Scene* was intended to serve as a "type" in a larger composition, much like this detail in the *Madonna dei Bentivoglio* altarpiece.

daio's fresco *The Sacrifice of Zachariah*, in Santa Maria Novella in Florence, which similarly contains a marble sacrifice in its architecture.

The use of fictive architectural reliefs to contain biblical and pagan "types" seems particularly strong in Ferrarese and Bolognese painting: for example, in Roberti's *Pala di San Lazzaro* and *Pala Portuense*, and in at least six of Lorenzo Costa's works, the most notable being his *Madonna dei Bentivoglio* in the Bolognese church of San Giacomo Maggiore (figs. 20–21).[23] In addition to the examples found in Roberti's work — perhaps the most obvious source for Maineri — one should also note the use of inset scenes in both the Madonna's throne and in the architecture of the National Gallery's *Pala Strozzi*, particularly since several scholars have suggested that it is precisely in these sections that one sees a record of Maineri's original composition most clearly.[24]

Before we can determine whether the *Sacrificial Scene* was a *modello* for an illusionistic "type" inset, we must consider the complexity of the drawing's architectural setting. Most insets have either a plain background or one painted with tesselated gold squares to create the effect of a gold-mosaic backing. The reason for this is two-fold: first, a highly detailed inset is difficult for the average viewer to read. The significance of the insets is nullified if they are impossible to understand. As a result, most are composed very simply, usually with just a ground line for the figures to stand on and the most minimal indications of setting. Second, if the insets are too detailed, they detract from the primacy of the main subject.

One painting attributed to Maineri clearly shows the consequences of architectural decoration getting out of hand. His *Flagellation of Christ* (fig. 22) is so busy with illusionistic details of putti, soldiers, horses, trophies, and inscriptions that the actual flagellation can barely compete for equal attention. Indeed, the excess of architectural decoration, made more oppressive by the strict symmetry of nearly every element, seems to subsume the purpose of the narrative altogether.

In the depiction of a Madonna and Child or of Christ the Redeemer, the "type" must be added discreetly, its message delivered *sotto voce* for the

devotional power of the image to remain intact. Having said that, however, the most notable exception to this rule appears in the *Pala Strozzi* itself. The bottom level of the Madonna's throne contains three fully-colored inset scenes. The central panel represents the *Massacre of the Innocents* (fig. 23). The figures are set within a shallow stage, very reminiscent of the *Sacrificial Scene*, and backed by a triumphal arch; yet the dramatic clarity of the event remains unimpinged. There is, therefore, a parallel for the architectural background of the *Sacrificial Scene* in a large-scale work directly related to Maineri. One suspects that, if the Art Institute drawing were translated into paint as an inset panel, its effect would be equally compelling and similarly effective.

Maineri's *Sacrificial Scene* is an important addition to the Art Institute's collection for several reasons. It is a superb drawing, among the finest to have survived from Renaissance Ferrara. It tells us a great deal, not only about the artistic styles and development of late fifteenth-century Ferrarese art, but also about the way one Ferrarese artist began the complex process of creating a work of art. And, finally, the *Sacrificial Scene* functions as an instructive cultural document. It records a fascinating moment in the development of the Italian Renaissance, when man was trying to reconcile the prerequisites of his predominantly Christian culture with his yearnings for the romance of his classical past.

FIGURE 22. Gian Francesco de' Maineri. *Flagellation of Christ*, 1490/99. Oil on panel; 35.5 x 25.4 cm. Formerly Milan, private collection.

FIGURE 23. Lorenzo Costa and Gian Francesco de' Maineri. Detail of figure 2 showing the *Massacre of the Innocents*.

Christ before Pilate: A Major Composition Study by Pontormo

LAURA M. GILES

Research Curator, Italian Drawings Catalogue
The Art Institute of Chicago

The Art Institute of Chicago recently enriched its collection of Italian drawings with the major acquisition of a black chalk composition study by Pontormo (1494–1557), one of the most extraordinary painters and draftsmen of sixteenth-century Florence (pl. 1 and fig. 1).[1] There are relatively few drawings by Pontormo outside the Galleria degli Uffizi in Florence, which possesses most of the over 400 drawings considered to be autograph;[2] as of this date, there are only fourteen Pontormo drawings in North American collections.[3] Hitherto unpublished, the Art Institute drawing was virtually unknown prior to its recent discovery in a private collection by Julien Stock, the first scholar to attribute it to Pontormo.[4] While the work's authenticity has been confirmed, its subject matter and precise function have hitherto been unidentified.[5] In addition to situating this highly enigmatic and expressive drawing within Pontormo's large graphic corpus, this article proposes to relate it to one of the artist's most important fresco projects on the basis of its style and content.

Baptized Jacopo Carucci, but known by the name of his small Tuscan birthplace (Pontorme, near Empoli), Pontormo moved to Florence around 1507. He studied briefly with Leonardo da Vinci, as well as with the lesser-known Mariotto Albertinelli and Piero di Cosimo, before working more extensively with Andrea del Sarto until 1514.[6] During his apprenticeship to these leading Florentine painters, he quickly absorbed the principles of High Renaissance style. As developed and perfected by Leonardo, this style fused into an harmonious whole the material and spiritual components of the human image, which had been treated separately by such fifteenth-century masters as Domenico Ghirlandaio and Sandro Bot-

ticelli. Using his extraordinary powers of imagination and empirical observation, Leonardo endowed his idealized figures with both physical immediacy and an otherworldly mystery.[7] To this classical language, several of the younger Florentine painters, and especially Andrea del Sarto, added a more visibly expressive element, characterized by a peculiar tension and excitability in the figures. Pontormo in turn exploited this quality in creating his highly personal vocabulary of beautifully composed, yet willfully distorted, forms.

Having mastered the newly evolved classical style, the young Pontormo broke with it dramatically in 1518 in the altarpiece of the *Madonna and Child with Saints* in the church of San Michele Visdomini in Florence (fig. 2). In this unsettling painting, Pontormo disrupted the peace and unity of a conventional Florentine High Renaissance composition with precariously balanced, unevenly lit, and extremely agitated figures who seem moved by irrational forces. During the next decade, Pontormo developed his mature style in several

FIGURE 1. Pontormo (Jacopo Carucci; Italian, 1494–1557). *Christ before Pilate* (detail of pl. 1), 1522/23. Black chalk, with stumping, and traces of red chalk, heightened with traces of white chalk, over incising, on cream laid paper; 27.4 x 28.3 cm. The Art Institute of Chicago, Restricted gift of Anne Searle Meers, the Regenstein Foundation, and Dr. William D. Shorey (1989.187). This drawing, recently discovered and attributed to the Florentine artist Pontormo, was probably executed as he was designing one of a number of frescoes he had been commissioned to execute for a Carthusian charterhouse outside Florence. The scene depicts an apocryphal event from the life of Christ, who is shown here with his hands bound behind him as he is led before the Roman procurator Pontius Pilate.

FIGURE 2. Pontormo. *Madonna and Child with Saints Joseph, John the Evangelist, Francis, James, and the Infant John the Baptist*, 1518. Oil on paper mounted on panel; 218 x 189 cm. Florence, San Michele Visdomini. Photo: Luciano Berti, *L'opera completa del Pontormo* (Milan, 1973), pl. 17. This unsettling and crowded altarpiece, with its agitated figures, marked Pontormo's first break with the classical style.

experimental works culminating in the lyrical and poignant *Entombment* altarpiece of 1526/27 in Santa Felicità (fig. 3), a work that, in its sculptural forms, reflects his intense and on-going study of Michelangelo.[8] Described by his contemporary and biographer Giorgio Vasari as "solitary beyond belief," during his lifetime Pontormo was both esteemed for his genius and criticized for his unconventional behavior and erratic working habits.[9] Throughout his career he was patronized by the Medici, the rulers of Florence, for whom he executed numerous portraits and frescoes. The latter range from the naturalistic *Vertumnus and Pomona* lunette of 1520/21 in the Medici villa of Poggio a Caiano (fig. 4) to the decoration of the choir of the family church of San Lorenzo in Florence, which Pontormo worked on in strict isolation from 1546 until his death. As revealed by the unidealized and weightless figures in one of the numerous extant preparatory studies for these frescoes (which were subsequently destroyed), Pontormo's later style became increasingly private and rarefied (fig. 5).

Together with his more radical compatriot Rosso Fiorentino, Pontormo forged the Mannerist style that

came to dominate Italian painting between 1520 and 1580, with its emphasis on eccentricity and refinement.[10] What clearly distinguishes Pontormo from Rosso and from subsequent Mannerists is the intensity of his emotional involvement with the subject matter. Rather than allow the form to exist merely for form's sake, Pontormo always balanced his aesthetic conception with his human response to the given content. In his *Entombment* altarpiece, for example, Pontormo has depicted himself as one of the grieving figures (in the upper right; fig. 3), thereby challenging the tradition whereby artists represented themselves in religious scenes as passive spectators.[11] Beyond the purely formal function it performs within the painting's taut circular design, this innovative self-portrait signifies Pontormo's active presence in the Entombment episode.

FIGURE 3. Pontormo. *Entombment*, 1526/27. Oil on panel; 313 x 192 cm. Florence, Santa Felicità. Photo: Florence, Gabinetto Fotografico, Soprintendenza Beni Artistici e Storici. Pontormo's mature, Mannerist style is evident in this tightly knit painting of the entombment of Christ. The artist has included a self-portrait in the upper right, thereby expressing his own emotional involvement in the event depicted.

FIGURE 4. Pontormo. *Vertumnus and Pomona*, 1520/21. Lunette fresco; 461 x 990 cm. Environs of Florence, Villa Poggio a Caiano. Photo: Berti, *L'opera completa del Pontormo*, pl. 29.

Pontormo's intense involvement with his subject matter is most strikingly illustrated in his drawings. He shared with all Florentine artists a belief in the fundamental role played by drawing in the creation of a work of art. The meaning of drawing, or *disegno*, incorporated the concept of artistic idea or design as well as that of actual execution. As defined by Vasari, *disegno* was "the father of our three arts, Architecture, Sculpture, and Painting."[12] By the middle of the fifteenth century a standard preparatory procedure had been established: the artist would first make a rough sketch (called *schizzo* or *primo pensiero*) of the composition, and then draw separate studies (or *studi*) of figures, different parts of the body, and drapery. These were integrated into a finished drawing (*disegno* or *modello*), which might then be squared for transfer and enlarged onto a cartoon (*cartone*) of the actual size of the fresco or panel painting.[13] With the exception of the cartoon (which was often destroyed in the process of transferring the design to the final surface), all of the standard preparatory types are represented in Pontormo's graphic oeuvre. Unlike most Florentine artists, however, Pontormo believed that drawing represented more than an intellectual concept or preparatory exercise. As for Leonardo and Michelangelo, drawing for Pontormo represented a means of deeply personal expression, thus becoming an end in itself.

Most of Pontormo's drawings are red and black chalk individual figure studies, many of which bear only an approximate relationship to a particular painting or fresco. In these studies Pontormo used his masterful understanding of human anatomy to highly expressive effect by deliberately distorting the figure in such a way

that it communicates the artist's emotional response to the subject, whether this be himself, as scrutinized in a mirror in a red chalk drawing in the British Museum (fig. 6), or a model in the studio, shown frontally and in profile in a black chalk sheet in the Fogg Art Museum (fig. 7). As conceived by Pontormo, the human figure becomes an abstract form charged with psychological content—one that is, in fact, often much more compelling in the drawing than that projected in the final painting or fresco. Such is the case with the Fogg drawing (fig. 7), which is a preliminary and subsequently abandoned study for the boy holding a staff to the right of the window in the center of the *Vertumnus and Pomona* fresco at Poggio a Caiano (fig. 4). In the drawing, Pontormo rendered the frontally posed nude model as a contorted and vulnerable creature, who strains towards us while shrinking back. Replaced by the more relaxed and contented boy in the fresco, this tense and hollow-eyed youth remains suspended in Pontormo's imagination—a work of art in its own right.

Several hollow-eyed and anxious faces recalling that of the model in the Fogg *Vertumnus and Pomona* study stare out at us from the Art Institute sheet, which is one of only about forty known composition studies (ranging from *primi pensieri* to *modelli*) by Pontormo. While several of these may be related to extant or documented works, the majority have been connected with lost or unexecuted projects. The Chicago drawing compares best stylistically with two examples from the second category which have been dated to the early and mid-1520s. One is a red chalk sheet in the Uffizi that represents the Adoration of the Magi (fig. 8). While its exact purpose is

FIGURE 5. Pontormo. *Composition Study for "Christ in Glory with the Creation of Eve,"* c. 1546/50. Black chalk; 32.6 x 18 cm. Florence, Galleria degli Uffizi (6609F). Photo: Florence, Gabinetto Fotografico, Soprintendenza Beni Artistici e Storici. This drawing, probably dating from the last decade of Pontormo's life, contrasts sharply with his more volumetric treatment of figures in the earlier *Christ before Pilate*.

FIGURE 6. Pontormo. *Male Nude (Self-Portrait)*, c. 1525. Red chalk; 28.4 x 20.2 cm. London, British Museum (1936–10–10–10r). Photo: London, British Museum. This wonderfully arresting self-portrait demonstrates Pontormo's ability to infuse his drawings with emotional and psychological content.

FIGURE 7. Pontormo. *Studies of a Nude Youth*, c. 1520. Black and red chalk; 43.5 x 28.5 cm. Cambridge, Mass., Fogg Art Museum, Harvard University, Bequest of Charles A. Loeser (1932.342).

GVARDA LA VERGIN CH' HVMILMENTE STASSI
IN PICCOLA CAPANNA, E'L FIGLIO ACCANTO,
COL FIDO SPOSO DAL CIEL VINTI, ET LASSI

unknown, it may well have been a preliminary idea for a nocturnal Nativity scene that, according to Vasari, Pontormo painted for the room of the Prior of the Certosa (or charterhouse) of San Lorenzo al Monte at Galluzzo, the Carthusian monastery outside Florence where the artist resided and worked between the end of 1522 and 1525.[14] A distinctive feature shared by the Art Institute and Uffizi drawings is the piling up of jumbled and elongated figures on either side of the composition. These forms are rendered with a variety of curving and angular contours and thick and spidery strokes, and then articulated with textured shadows and volumetric drapery folds. While each drawing has a relatively worked-up quality that distinguishes it from a sketchier *primo pensiero* (see fig. 11), the dense clusters of *pentimenti* (or changes) throughout reveal that there is much to be resolved in the compositions, particularly with regard to the spatial relationships, which appear to be in a state of flux. In the Art Institute drawing, the greatest area of uncertainty is in the center of the foreground, where a large kneeling figure and several other nebulous forms are superimposed on a flight of steps. Pontormo enlarged this kneeling figure, as is indicated by the smaller head and shoulders legible within the form (see pl. 7). Such an abrupt and unsettling change of scale also occurs in the horseman on the left of the second comparative composition drawing (fig. 9). Executed in black chalk and almost identical in size and format to the Art Institute drawing, this study has been dated 1522/25 by Janet Cox-Rearick, who identified the subject matter as the Israelites drinking water in the wilderness.[15] Here Pontormo has revised his composition more extensively than in the Art Institute drawing, reworking the spindly figures to the point of ghostly illegibility.

In creating such blurred and shifting forms, Pontormo was following Leonardo's method of making rough sketches as an aid to artistic invention. This method challenged established Florentine workshop practice, which placed a premium on a careful and unerased line. In his *Treatise on Painting*, Leonardo discouraged such practice, proposing instead that one should sketch an "untidy composition," which was anal-

FIGURE 9. Pontormo. *Composition Study for Israelites Drinking the Water in the Wilderness*, 1522/25. Black chalk heightened with white, squared in black chalk; 28.5 x 28.3 cm. Florence, Uffizi (6675F.) Photo: Florence, Gabinetto Fotografico, Soprintendenza Beni Artistici e Storici. The Galleria degli Uffizi in Florence houses over 400 Pontormo drawings, among which is this black chalk drawing that has also been dated to the same period as *Christ before Pilate*. Here Pontormo has reworked his figures so extensively, shaping them and shifting their relative positions and scale, that the scene is virtually indecipherable.

FIGURE 8. Pontormo. *Composition Study for an Adoration of the Magi*, c. 1522. Red chalk; 47.5 x 31.4 cm. Florence, Uffizi (436S). Photo: Florence, Gabinetto Fotografico, Soprintendenza Beni Artistici e Storici. This drawing, like the Art Institute's *Christ before Pilate*, shows how Pontormo crowded his composition with elongated figures that he worked over repeatedly in his effort to resolve the inherent complications of spatial relationships. Dating from the same period as the Art Institute's drawing, this composition may have been a preparatory work for an unrealized painting also intended for the Carthusian monastery at Galluzzo.

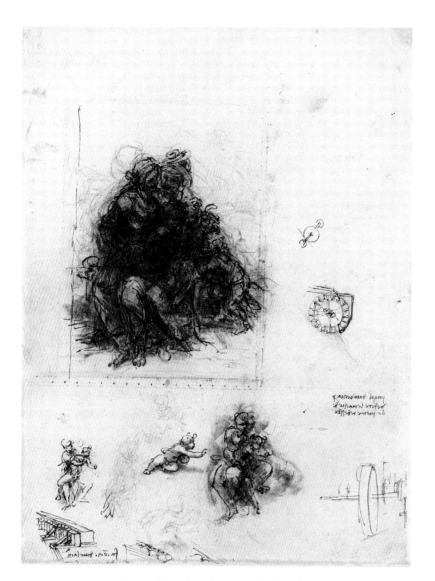

FIGURE 10. Leonardo da Vinci (Italian, 1452–1519). *Study for the "Virgin and Child with Saint Anne and the Infant Saint John the Baptist" and Studies of Machinery*, 1503/06. Pen and brown ink and gray wash (heightened with white in principal study) over black chalk; 26.7 x 20.1 cm. London, British Museum (1875–6–12–7). Pontormo's drawing procedure, as shown in several of the preceding illustrations, owed something to Leonardo's principle of using an "untidy composition" as a stimulus to further refinement.

ogous to a poet's first draft, before further refining the design.[16] Leonardo's revolutionary procedure is exemplified in a black chalk study in the British Museum for the cartoon of the *Virgin and Child with Saint Anne and the Infant Saint John the Baptist* in the National Gallery, London (fig. 10). In this study the swirling *pentimenti* became so confused that Leonardo later had to trace through the most essential lines to the verso with a stylus in order to transfer to another sheet the design he wished to preserve.[17] A similar intent is indicated in the incised lines in the *Israelites* study, the verso of which Pontormo blackened in certain areas for transfer to another sheet.

In order to understand the stylistic reasons for placing both the study for the *Adoration of the Magi* and the study for the *Israelites Drinking the Water in the Wilderness* in the early and mid-1520s, it is helpful to compare them with one slightly earlier and another considerably

later example, which have been related to extant or documented projects. The first of these, a black chalk study for the Visdomini altarpiece of 1518 (fig. 11), is even more roughly executed than the Art Institute study and is clearly a *primo pensiero* for the final work (fig. 2). As in all of Pontormo's drawings, there is a typically Florentine emphasis on line, here exemplified in the angular and rounded strokes and contours, which both create the underlying pyramidal design and define the figures. At the same time, there is a subtle but significant difference in the quality of the contour, which is consistently broader in the Visdomini study than in the Uffizi examples, wherein the line frequently becomes brittle and ragged. In the Visdomini study, Pontormo used sweeping curves and slashing angles to construct weightier figures, which twist and turn more aggressively in space than do their more constricted and compressed counterparts in the Uffizi examples. By contrast, if we turn to a black chalk composition study for one of the late San Lorenzo frescoes, *Christ in Glory with the Creation of Eve* (fig. 5), there is a complete absence of weight in this vision of transparent serpentine shapes floating in a void. At once more volumetric than these forms and yet less substantial than the figures in the Visdomini study, the shadowy presences in the studies for the *Adoration of the Magi* and the *Israelites* represent an intermediary stage in Pontormo's constantly changing and increasingly immaterial conception of the human figure.

Unlike the two Uffizi composition studies discussed earlier, the Art Institute drawing may be related to an extant work also from the 1520s. This is *Christ before Pilate* (fig. 12), Pontormo's only known depiction of this scene and one of five fresco lunettes illustrating scenes from the Passion, which Pontormo executed between 1523 and 1524 during his stay at the Certosa del Galluzzo outside of Florence.[18] According to Vasari, Pontormo seized the opportunity to flee a slight outbreak of the

plague in Florence in the fall of 1522 when he was called on by the Prior of the Certosa to execute a fresco cycle in the monastery's large cloister, which had been completed in 1516.[19] Now housed in the Certosa's museum, the ruined frescoes were detached from the cloister walls in 1955/56 to prevent further deterioration.

Founded in 1342 by Niccolò Acciaiuoli, a member of a prominent Florentine banking dynasty, the Certosa del Galluzzo was one of the most important Italian centers of the Carthusian monastic order, which, in contrast to the more actively apostolic Dominican and Franciscan orders, was purely contemplative.[20] Carthusians devoted themselves to the direction of souls through liturgical celebrations in the choir and spiritual exercises done in isolation. Vasari noted that the monastery's solitude and silence suited Pontormo's temperament, so much so that he prolonged his work on the frescoes, and continued to visit the Certosa after his return to Florence.[21]

Along with the decoration of the San Lorenzo choir, the Certosa fresco cycle has always been considered to

FIGURE 11. Pontormo. *Composition Study for the "Visdomini Altarpiece,"* c. 1518. Black chalk heightened with white on pink prepared paper; 21.8 x 16 cm. Rome, Gabinetto Nazionale delle Stampe (F.C.147). Photo: Kurt W. Forster, *Pontormo: Monographie mit Kritischem Katalog* (Munich, 1966), fig. 13.

FIGURE 12. Pontormo. *Christ before Pilate*, 1523/24. Lunette fresco, 300 x 290 cm. Florence, Museo della Certosa del Galluzzo. Photo: Florence, Gabinetto Fotografico, Soprintendenza Beni Artistici e Storici. This fresco is one of the five that Pontormo executed for the large cloister in the monastery at Galluzzo. The final arrangement of the figures here differs greatly from that in the Art Institute study.

FIGURE 13. Albrecht Dürer (German, 1471–1528). *Christ before Herod (The Small Passion)*, 1509. Woodcut; 12.8 x 9.8 cm. The Art Institute of Chicago, Clarence Buckingham Collection (1951.117). The German master Albrecht Dürer exercised a powerful influence on numerous Italian artists, and certainly the example afforded by his series of woodcut illustrations known as the *Small Passion* deeply affected Pontormo's handling of his own composition of *Christ before Pilate*.

represent the most extreme of Pontormo's stylistic experiments. His contemporaries believed that in these works Pontormo had betrayed his Florentine heritage by turning to the prints of the German master Albrecht Dürer as a major source of inspiration. While other Florentine artists, including Andrea del Sarto, had quoted extensively from Dürer, none had allowed their style to be so deeply affected. Vasari concluded that

the charm of his own [Pontormo's] early manner, which had been given to him by nature, all full of sweetness and grace, suffered a great change from that new study and labour, and was so impaired through his stumbling on that German manner, that in all these works, though they are all beautiful, there is but a sorry remnant to be seen of that excellence and grace that he had given up to that time to all his figures.[22]

The attenuated figures, crowded groupings, and elaborate drapery patterns in the Certosa frescoes indeed reflect Pontormo's careful study of Dürer's prints, especially of the woodcuts in the *Small Passion* of 1511. Clearly, the impact of these works, together with the austere and meditative environment of the Certosa, and Pontormo's personal response to the subject matter, helped produce a style that in its compressed spaces, flattened shapes, and overall dreamlike effect was worlds apart from the buoyant illusionism of *Vertumnus and*

FIGURE 14. Donatello (Italian, 1386[?]-1466). *Christ before Pilate* (detail), 1460/66. Bronze relief; 137 x 280 cm (pulpit). Florence, San Lorenzo, north pulpit. Photo: H.W. Janson, *The Sculpture of Donatello* (Princeton, N.J., 1957), vol. 1, fig. 389. Donatello's bronze relief from a pulpit in the church of San Lorenzo influenced Pontormo's arrangement of figures within an architectural setting and his resolution of the confrontation between Christ and Pilate.

Pomona, executed only a few years earlier.

In the Art Institute study for *Christ before Pilate*, Pontormo experimented with a highly unusual illustration of the scene that he abandoned in the fresco itself. There, the bound Christ stands at center in profile and with bowed head before Pilate, who is likewise conventionally portrayed as seated in judgment and about to wash his hands, using the basin and pitcher brought by the page descending the central staircase. Placed off center in the Art Institute drawing and with his back turned to us, Christ is identifiable as the tall standing figure on the left with his hands tied behind his back. He holds his head erect and looks up at Pilate, the shrinking and stooping figure at the top of the stairs, who turns towards us as he grasps the round handles of a portal. In spite of these differences, both fresco and drawing share

important compositional features: among these are the bound figure of Christ, the central axis (provided by the stairs in the fresco and by the doors and short flight of steps in the drawing), and the roughly symmetrical groups of figures crowded on either side of this axis. In addition, if one studies the lower part of the drawing, one can see Pontormo's first thoughts for the half-length soldiers looming up from below in the fresco in the hunched, three-quarter-length figure in the lower left corner who holds onto Christ, and also in the inchoate shapes superimposed on the staircase. Finally, it is possible to discern in the upper left portion of the drawing two ornate pikes or halberds (one erect, the other on a diagonal), which are similar to those carried by several of the soldiers in the lunette.

Although there are no specific documented payments for *Christ before Pilate*, Vasari indicated that it was the second fresco that Pontormo executed in the Certosa Passion cycle.[23] In his description of *Christ before Pilate*, Vasari noted the extremely Germanic appearance of several of the soldiers, which he contrasted with the "life-like and very beautiful" page boy, who alone has "something of the old manner of Jacopo."[24] Although Pontormo did draw inspiration from Dürer's woodcuts for the poses and outfits of many of the soldiers, as well as for the crowding of Christ by the soldiers (fig. 13),[25] he was also deeply indebted to an earlier Florentine source for the composition as a whole and for the relationship between Christ and Pilate. As Irving Lavin has demonstrated, Donatello's bronze relief of the same subject, from one of two pulpits in the church of San Lorenzo that he worked on between 1460 and his death in 1466 (fig. 14), provided Pontormo with several key elements: the poses of Christ and Pilate, the unusual inclusion of Pilate's wife, the soldiers at the bottom of the lunette (who derive from the slumbering half-length armed guards in the relief), and finally the deep architectural background.[26]

In her recent study of Pontormo's Passion cycle, Paula Beckers proposed that the devotional and iconographical source for the Certosa frescoes was a text fundamental to the purely contemplative spirit of the Carthusian order.[27] This was the fourteenth-century *Vita Christi*, written by the Carthusian monk Ludolph of Saxony. First printed in 1474, it was one of the most widely read books of the late fifteenth century, and archi-

val records indicate that it was almost certainly acquired for the Certosa's richly endowed library in 1483.[28] The purpose of this work was to provide a sequence of meditations that, through an exhaustive commentary on the Gospels and subsequent spiritual texts, present Christ as the perfect ideal of sanctity to which humanity should aspire. The first part of the *Vita* concerns the public ministry of Christ, while the second part consists of meditations on his Passion, which are arranged according to the periods of the eight canonical hours regulating the monastic day. In addition to proposing that the content of Pontormo's frescoes is based on Ludolph's work, Beckers has argued that the frescoes themselves and their placement in the corners of the large cloister of the Certosa fulfilled a key devotional function in the monks' daily canonical schedule. Situated along the route taken by the monks between their cells and the chapel, the frescoes would have served as monumental meditational texts for them to contemplate between the two principal Carthusian activities: liturgical celebration and solitary devotion.

Although the *Vita Christi* may well have been the principal iconographical source for the Certosa frescoes, its conventional account of the scene with Christ before Pilate does not include the episode that Pontormo

FIGURE 15. Pontormo. *Composition Study for "Vertumnus and Pomona,"* c. 1520. Pen and brown ink and wash over black chalk; 19.8 x 38 cm. Florence, Uffizi (454F.) Photo: Florence, Gabinetto Fotografico, Soprintendenza Beni Artistici e Storici.

chose to illustrate in the Art Institute study. This episode is not mentioned in any of the four evangelical Gospels. It was first described in the apocryphal fourth-century Gospel of Nicodemus, or Acts of Pilate, and later adapted in a late fifteenth-century Italian devotional work, *Meditatione sopra la passione del nostro signore iesu christo*. This passion tract derived from the widely read *Meditationes vitae Christi*, considered to be the work of a thirteenth-century Franciscan monk known as pseudo-Bonaventura. Likewise attributed to pseudo-Bonaventura, the *Meditatione* was an extremely popular work, as is indicated by the twenty-eight editions that were printed in Italy between c. 1478 and 1500.[29] According to the relevant passage in the *Meditatione*, when Christ entered the Roman governor's palace, twelve imperial standards held by ensigns lowered themselves of their own accord in homage to Christ, whereupon all of those assembled were compelled to kneel in worship. Beholding this spectacle, Pilate became afraid and left the room.[30] It is Pilate's fearful exit that is specified in the *Meditatione* and that becomes the formal and psychological focus of Pontormo's illustration of the scene.[31] Pontormo created this focus by placing Pilate approximately at the center of the composition and by diminishing the size of his horrified face in relation to the rest of his body (see pl. 6). He thereby achieved an optical distortion that is at once disturbing and compelling, and analogous to the distortion that occurs in Pontormo's radically foreshortened self-portrait drawing (fig. 6). In addition, Pontormo juxtaposes the cowering Pilate with the columnar Christ, whose large spherical head contrasts with Pilate's shrunken one.

In the absence of any detailed documentation on the Certosa frescoes, one can only speculate why Pontormo's apocryphal conception of the scene of Christ before Pilate was abandoned in the transition from drawing to fresco. Whatever external reasons there may have been for the iconographical transformation, such a radical change between preliminary idea and final product is entirely characteristic of Pontormo's preparatory process. A striking example is provided by comparing Pontormo's earliest extant idea for the *Vertumnus and Pomona* fresco, as preserved in a composition study in the Uffizi, with the finished work (fig. 4). In this drawing (fig. 15), Pontormo packed the lunette space with sprawling muscular figures, unquestionably inspired by those in Michelangelo's Sistine ceiling. Presumably deeming this monumental conception unsuitable for the fresco's poetic subject matter and the villa's bucolic setting, Pontormo replaced it with one that was more human and naturalistic.[32] The numerous figure studies related to the final design of the *Vertumnus and Pomona* confirm Vasari's account of how Pontormo constantly revised his ideas

FIGURE 16. Pontormo. *Composition Study for the "Entombment,"* c. 1526/27. Black chalk heightened with white, with brown wash, squared in red chalk; 44.5 x 27.6 cm. Oxford, Christ Church Library (1336). By permission of the Governing Body, Christ Church, Oxford.

FIGURE 17. Pontormo. *Composition Study for a Deposition*, c. 1524. Red chalk; 12.6 x 10 cm. Florence, Uffizi (6622F.) Photo: Florence, Gabinetto Fotografico, Soprintendenza Beni Artistici e Storici.

while working on the fresco, thereby prolonging its execution: "destroying and doing over again everyday what he had done the day before, he racked his brains in such a manner that it was a tragedy; but all the time he was always making new discoveries, which brought credit to himself and beauty to the work."[33]

As we have already seen, the multiple layers of fluctuating ideas in the Art Institute drawing suggest a similar creative struggle. In addition, the study demonstrates how Pontormo worked out an overall design, using various formal and technical means to attain expressive ends. As in many of his completed works, he compressed the foreground figures toward us while sealing off the background, thus blurring the distinction made by High Renaissance artists between our own space and that of the painting. Here we are brought close to the masses of shifting forms, which are dramatically modeled with a flickering light. Certain figures (most notably Christ, Pilate, and the kneeling figure in the right foreground) are distinguished by broader areas of light and shadow, the latter created by stumping or smudging the black chalk in such a way as to allow the tonality of the paper to filter through (see the accompanying article by Harriet K. Stratis for further discussion of this and related issues). As a result, the surface has an overall transparent and luminous texture that is ultimately mysterious in nature and reinforces the enigmatic quality of the scene. This luminosity also distinguishes the slightly later, and more finished, composition study for the *Entombment* altarpiece of 1526/27, where the figures have become more sculptural and graceful, and the overall effect less agitated (fig. 16). Indeed, in this work Pontormo achieved the perfect balance between eccentric form and classical order that he experimented with in the Art Institute study.

Whereas one can trace the complex evolution of Pontormo's *Vertumnus and Pomona* in approximately thirty extant preparatory studies,[34] such documentation is lacking for *Christ before Pilate*, and for the Certosa frescoes as a whole. Only nineteen studies have been related to the entire cycle.[35] Predominantly figure studies, none of these relates to *Christ before Pilate*,[36] and only two qualify as composition studies. It is, however, extremely useful to compare them with the Art Institute drawing. Both in the Uffizi, these studies are related to two unexecuted lunette frescoes: a *Deposition* (which Vasari mentions, along with a *Crucifixion*), and a *Nailing to the Cross*.[37] Apart from the clearly indicated arched picture space and the dependence on relevant woodcuts from Dürer's *Small Passion*,[38] the two drawings are extremely different from each other in media and technique, degree of finish, and overall effect. The *Deposition* study (fig. 17) is a small and summary red chalk sketch, its schematized yet eloquent figures composed simply of sweeping contours and broad parallel hatching. Executed in black chalk with some white heightening, the other study (fig. 18) is more fully realized: the facial features of the spindly and agitated figures are articulated, and there is some indication of internal modeling. In both works, however, there is a distinctively flat and patterned effect that may be attributed to the influence of Dürer's prints, and that is less apparent in the Art Institute drawing. These Uffizi studies have been placed by Cox-Rearick

towards the middle of the Certosa period.[39] The more rounded and volumetric forms and deeper space of the Art Institute drawing, which resemble those of the *Adoration of the Magi* study, suggest that it belongs to a different, and probably earlier, stylistic moment, when Dürer's influence on Pontormo was less pervasive. Several elements in the Art Institute drawing indicate that at this early stage in the evolution of the Certosa frescoes Pontormo turned to a quintessentially Florentine High Renaissance source, which he then modified somewhat through his study of Dürer's prints.

This source was Andrea del Sarto's fresco decoration of the Chiostro dello Scalzo, the courtyard of a secular Florentine confraternity.[40] Originally built as a simple, flat, timber-roofed atrium, with a low stone bench running all round the wall, the courtyard was considerably altered in 1722 with the addition of vaults and arches. Del Sarto worked on these frescoes, with several interruptions, from about 1511 until 1526. Considered to be the most important decorative project of the Florentine High Renaissance, the Chiostro murals would have been a likely model for Pontormo to consult when designing the Certosa fresco cycle. The painted ensemble in the Chiostro dello Scalzo consisted of twelve rectangular grisaille (or monochrome) frescoes illustrating the life of

FIGURE 18. Pontormo. *Composition Study for a Nailing to the Cross*, c. 1523/24. Black chalk heightened with white, squared in red chalk; 17.3 x 16.5 cm. Florence, Uffizi (6671F.) Photo: Florence, Gabinetto Fotografico, Soprintendenza Beni Artistici e Storici. Both this composition study and the preceding one can be dated slightly later than the Art Institute's *Christ before Pilate*. These two drawings are also distinctively flat and much simpler in design. These attributes probably reflect the increasing influence that Dürer's woodcuts had on Pontormo.

FIGURE 19. Andrea del Sarto (Italian, 1486–1530). *Arrest of Saint John the Baptist*, 1517. Fresco; 191 x 312 cm. Florence, Chiostro dello Scalzo. Photo: Florence, Gabinetto Fotografico, Soprintendenza Beni Artistici e Storici. If Pontormo found any Florentine mural cycles particularly influential, it was more than likely the ensemble of frescoes that Andrea del Sarto produced for the courtyard of a local confraternity. The example shown here clearly suggested to Pontormo a way to bring Christ into confrontation with Pilate, employing the same spatial relationship that the centrally placed Herod has with the bystander to the left of this fresco.

Saint John the Baptist, four illusionistic statues of the four cardinal Virtues, and a fictive architectural framework that both harmonized with and enhanced the rectilinear and horizontal character of the setting. In the resulting masterful union of painting, sculpture, and architecture, del Sarto added a new illusionistic dimension to the tradition of monumental Florentine fresco decoration. Also unprecedented was the utter simplicity of the boxlike architectural settings of many of the scenes, and the monumental scale of the figures, both of which became increasingly classical during the fifteen-year span of the project.

By the time of the date of the first recorded payment to Pontormo for his work in the cloister of the Certosa, del Sarto had painted five of the ten narrative scenes he would eventually execute (two others were done by Franciabigio). Of these, it is the *Arrest of Saint John the Baptist* of 1517 (fig. 19) that appears to serve as the key point of departure for Pontormo's initial conception of the *Christ before Pilate* lunette. More austere in its setting and more rigidly symmetrical than the previous frescoes in the Chiostro, the *Arrest* itself, as John Shearman has argued, is largely based on Raphael's tapestry cartoon *The Blinding of Elymas*, which was executed the year before and publicized immediately through an engraving by Agostino Veneziano.[41] Not only is the composition derivative, but del Sarto has also borrowed several motifs from Raphael's work. One of these is the dignified bystander on the left, who derives from the back view of Saint Paul. This figure became the basis for the columnar Christ in Pontormo's drawing, bearing approximately the same spatial relationship to Pilate that the bystander does to Herod in the *Arrest of Saint John the Baptist*. Also echoed in the Art Institute drawing is the stagelike setting with a severely centralized architectural focus, which Pontormo reinforced with the vertical ruled lines denoting the embrasure of the doors. Finally, the absence in the drawing of an arched top (such as is found in the two Uffizi composition studies for the *Deposition* and *Nailing to the Cross*) would indicate that at this stage Pontormo was not yet conceiving of the Certosa frescoes as lunettes—the most viable format for the walls of the arched and vaulted Chiostro Grande—but was simply experimenting with the rectilinear model provided by Andrea del Sarto in the Chiostro dello Scalzo.

As suggested earlier, Pontormo modified this model by turning to Dürer's prints. Of these, it is the *Ascension* woodcut in the *Small Passion* (fig. 20) that is recalled most specifically in the Art Institute drawing.[42] The two kneeling figures in the foreground appear to derive from the pair of kneeling saints in the foreground of the print. As in the woodcut, they function as the base of an inverted arc of figures that hug three sides of the composition. In thus creating a crowded foreground and ambiguous space, Pontormo substantially altered del Sarto's austere setting and overtly geometric design.

In the absence of other extant preparatory drawings, it is difficult to trace the evolution of Pontormo's design for *Christ before Pilate* between the Art Institute study and the Certosa lunette. It is clear that in the fresco Pontormo rejected del Sarto's classical style and proposed a more crowded and expressive alternative, made largely in response to Dürer and Donatello. Even more emphatically than in the Art Institute drawing, in the

FIGURE 20. Albrecht Dürer. *The Ascension (The Small Passion)*, 1509/11. Woodcut; 12.5 x 7.8 cm. The Art Institute of Chicago, The Clarence Buckingham Collection (1951.117). The two kneeling saints in this print by Dürer offered Pontormo an excellent model for his introduction of similar figures in his *Christ before Pilate*.

FIGURE 21. Pontormo. *Visitation*, 1514/16. Fresco; 392 x 337 cm. Florence, SS. Annunziata. Photo: Florence, Gabinetto Fotografico, Soprintendenza Beni Artistici e Storici.

final work Pontormo substituted eccentric shapes and abrupt transitions for del Sarto's naturalistic forms and measured intervals, and eliminated the traditional distinction between our own space and that of the painting, which del Sarto maintained in his stagelike settings.

In light of the connection proposed here between the Art Institute drawing and the frescoes in the Chiostro dello Scalzo, it is pertinent that the Certosa lunettes were the first large-scale narrative religious works that Pontormo executed after the *Visitation* fresco (1514/16) in the courtyard of SS. Annunziata, a decorative project to which Andrea del Sarto and Rosso contributed (fig. 21). In comparing the drawing with the fresco, it is apparent that Pontormo has used the more classical composition of the earlier fresco as a point of departure, retaining the centralized and symmetrical composition with steps, but compressing more figures into a more constricted space. It should also be noted that there is a specific reference in the Art Institute drawing to the less classical, but still centralized, Visdomini altarpiece in the pairs of putti that seem to embrace pilasters on either side of the door. These recall, both in their symmetrical placement and quasi-sculptural quality, the two energetic putti bearing the canopy above the Virgin and Child (fig. 2).

In his discussion of the Certosa frescoes, Vasari wrote that "Pontormo thought with such an occasion to make a special effort in the matters of art, and to show to the world that he had acquired greater perfection and a different manner since those works that he had executed before."[43] While there is no question that in creating this "different manner" Pontormo consciously borrowed from and imitated Dürer, he was also responding to the most recent developments in Florentine painting. As is demonstrated in the experimental Art Institute drawing, at this particular moment Pontormo was both emulating and challenging the classical manner being developed by Andrea del Sarto in his Chiostro dello Scalzo frescoes. The drawing is thus a vital document of the formative years of Italian Mannerism, illustrating how one of its founders worked within and broke away from the Florentine High Renaissance tradition by manipulating its classical principles for expressive ends. Beyond its significance within Pontormo's stylistic development, this probing work dramatically reveals the evolving design of a deeply personal vision. It captures the essence of Pontormo's introspective approach to the given content, one that combines the human and spiritual elements in a compelling image that is both otherworldly and immediate.

PLATE 1. Pontormo (Jacopo Carucci; Italian, 1494–1557). *Christ before Pilate*, 1522/23. Black chalk, with stumping, and traces of red chalk, heightened with traces of white chalk, over incising, on cream laid paper; 27.4 x 28.3 cm. The Art Institute of Chicago, Restricted gift of Anne Searle Meers, the Regenstein Foundation, and Dr. William D. Shorey (1989.187).

Following pages:
PLATE 2. Gian Francesco de' Maineri (Italian, active 1489–1506). *Sacrificial Scene*, 1489/90. Pen and black ink, with brush and gray and brown wash, heightened with lead white (partially discolored), on cream laid paper; 41.8 x 20 cm. The Art Institute of Chicago, Regenstein Collection (1989.686).

PLATE 3. Giovanni Benedetto Castiglione (Italian, 1609–1664). *God Creating Adam*, c. 1645. Monotype in black ink on ivory laid paper (dark-ground manner); 30.2 x 20.5 cm. The Art Institute of Chicago, Restricted gift of Dr. and Mrs. William D. Shorey and promised gift of an anonymous donor (1985.1113).

PLATE 5. Rosalba Carriera (Italian, 1675–1757). *Young Lady with a Parrot*, c. 1730. Pastel on blue laid paper; 59.8 x 50 cm. Helen Regenstein Collection (1985.43).

PLATE 4. Federico Barocci (Italian, 1535–1612). *Christ Child: Study for the "Madonna di San Giovanni,"* c. 1565. Black and red chalk, with pastel and stumping, on greenish-blue laid paper; 40.1 x 26.3 cm. The Art Institute of Chicago, Gift of Mrs. William F. E. Gurley (1990.512.1).

PLATE 6. Pontormo. *Christ before Pilate* (detail of pl. 1). Pilate, shown here in detail, was drawn to a much smaller scale in black chalk than was originally indicated by the incising. His head in particular was significantly reduced when the artist deviated from the incised underdrawing in black chalk.

PLATE 7. Pontormo. *Christ before Pilate* (detail of pl. 1). Initially, this kneeling figure to Pilate's immediate left was much smaller and the contours of the form closely followed the incising. Pontormo then reworked his composition and substantially enlarged the figure, creating a dramatic change in scale.

PLATE 8. Pontormo. *Christ before Pilate* (detail of pl. 1). This grouping of figures was superimposed over a partially incised set of stairs as a later modification to the composition.

The Technical Aspects of Pontormo's
Christ before Pilate

HARRIET K. STRATIS

Andrew W. Mellon Fellow in Paper Conservation
The Art Institute of Chicago

Pontormo's composition study *Christ before Pilate* is a drawing of great visual ambiguity. The superposition of both architectural details and figures of various size allows no clear reading of a single space. The artist's placement of two or more forms in the same physical space necessarily implies a working method in which layers of chalk are applied over one another to modify and redefine various passages. Often the result of this layered application of media confuses rather than informs the unaided eye. Visual evidence augmented by a comprehensive technical investigation involving stereomicroscopy and infrared reflectography may be used to decipher these forms, and to come to an understanding of the artist's application and manipulation of his drawing materials.

For Pontormo, drawing provided the most immediate and spontaneous course by which he could give expression to his artistic sensibilities. The result is an interaction of stylistic intention and artistic process. Style, technique, and materials are combined in *Christ before Pilate* to transform an untouched sheet of paper from a flat monochromatic surface to a picture plane that opens onto a deep architectural space crowded with figures. The transformation is achieved by means of the drawn line, whose characteristics are determined by the nature of the material chosen to create it, and by the pressure and movement of the artist's hand in applying this material to paper.

The tone and surface texture of a given sheet of paper are also essential to the artist's realization of his stylistic intention. Pontormo most often chose papers that were white to cream in tonality, although he occasionally used colored papers as well.[1] The Art Institute composition study is executed on a cream antique-laid paper. It is a light-to-medium-weight paper that has a hard, lightly textured surface. A sheet of laid paper is made using a fine wire screen, or paper mold. The wire network of the paper mold is constructed with parallel rows of thin wires placed very close together, crossed at larger intervals by thicker wires placed at right angles. Often, as in this drawing, the laid and chain lines (formed by the thinner and thicker wires, respectively) impart a surface texture to the sheet which is legible beneath the drawing media. In this sheet of paper, the chain lines are set rather far apart, 4.2 to 4.3 centimeters, and the laid lines usually number ten per centimeter.

Various watermarks have been documented in the papers used by Pontormo, and all are of Italian origin. Three of the most common include the Latin cross, the Greek cross, and the acorn sprig. When the Art Institute drawing is viewed in transmitted light, an acorn sprig watermark can be seen slightly left of center (fig. 1). The watermark is composed of a central acorn flanked by two oak leaves on either side of a stem. The "stem" also happens to be the chain line that runs directly through the center of the watermark. For the purposes of this study and for comparison with other similar watermarks, an exact impression of the watermark was transferred through beta-radiography onto x-ray film and a contact print created (fig. 2). The watermark is of incontestably Italian, and probably Florentine, origin, according to Briquet, who recorded a nearly identical watermark found on a Florentine document dated 1530.[2] It can also be found in a sheet of studies by Michelangelo tentatively dated to the late 1520s.[3] Ten Pontormo drawings are known to have an acorn sprig watermark, and all of these

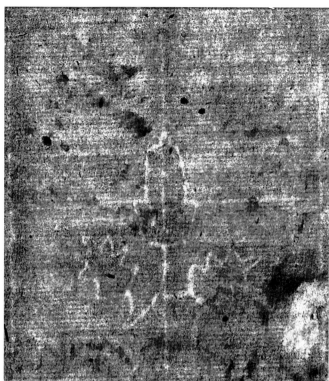

FIGURE 1. Pontormo. *Christ before Pilate* (detail of pl. 1). Photo: Harriet K. Stratis. This detail of the drawing, photographed in transmitted light, reveals the relative placement of the acorn sprig watermark with respect to Pilate's hands in the upper right and to the two kneeling figures to Pilate's immediate left. This same watermark has been documented in ten other drawings by Pontormo and in a work by Michelangelo, all from the 1520s.

FIGURE 2. Beta-radiography was used to record the acorn sprig watermark found in Pontormo's *Christ before Pilate*. The watermark has been reproduced here in its actual size with the chain lines at either side. Its placement in the drawing can best be understood by comparison with figure 1. Beta-radiograph: Harriet K. Stratis.

have been dated between 1519 and 1525. The existence of this watermark in *Christ before Pilate* places the drawing squarely within the period when Pontormo used this particular paper for five studies for *Vertumnus and Pomona* (1520/21) and for one study of *The Israelites Drinking the Water in the Wilderness* (1522/25), as well as for four additional sheets of studies (1519/21).[4]

Pontormo favored red and black chalk in his drawings, perhaps because of their versatility and their ease of manipulation. The chalk could be applied directly to draw straight or curved lines, and horizontal, vertical, or diagonal hatching. To create thinner passages of powdered chalk, the friable medium could be stumped, or smudged on the paper. As a result, the artist could estab-

lish contrasts of light and dark and create volumetric forms.[5] In *Christ before Pilate*, the layered nature of Pontormo's drawing method, from the underdrawing to the uppermost layer of stumped chalk, contributes to a rich but difficult composition. A systematic examination of each of these layers helps to establish the precise techniques used by the artist.

Throughout this composition study, there is a network of heavily incised lines that clearly parallel many of the forms articulated in black chalk. Incised lines can be made in a sheet of paper using a stylus and are often clearly legible even where they are devoid of media. In most cases, incising is a method used to transfer a composition, wholly or in part, onto a second sheet of paper to be further elaborated upon. Often the verso of the sheet to be incised is blackened with chalk so that during the transfer process the chalk fills the newly incised lines on the second sheet, enhancing their legibility. In *Christ before Pilate*, however, the verso of the sheet is not blackened as it most likely would have been had the drawing been used as a matrix for transfer. Nor were any black chalk passages transferred onto the recto of the drawing from a second sheet of paper, since black chalk particles do not consistently fill and follow the contours of the incised lines. While other possible transfer techniques have been considered,[6] it is most likely that the incised lines were applied directly to the drawing surface as part of the process used by Pontormo to establish the preliminary composition, using the stylus freely to create an underdrawing (pl. 6 and fig. 3). With the incised lines as a foundation, Pontormo continued his composition study in black chalk, and in the process deviated from his underdrawing by altering compositional forms. Where lines were deeply incised, the chalk could be drawn over them without depositing particles of chalk in the incising. For this reason, most of Pontormo's stylus underdrawing remains visible. Where lines were more superficially incised, black chalk particles filled the incised lines, obscuring them. This is particularly true in the stumped passages.

The technique of using a stylus underdrawing to establish an initial composition that is subsequently realized in chalk is not unique to Pontormo. Raphael often began his chalk studies by first using a stylus to create a composition, as in his black chalk study of *Poetry* for the vault of the Stanza della Segnatura, a drawing now in the Royal Library, Windsor (fig. 4).[7] In this study, the stylus was used to create a well-defined underdrawing. The incised composition was changed slightly when Raphael proceeded in black chalk, yet the proportions initially established were more or less maintained. In contrast, Pontormo used the stylus underdrawing in his study as a point of departure from which he could make dramatic compositional changes.

In *Christ before Pilate* a comparison of the incised forms with their corresponding chalk-drawn forms clearly reveals that the figure of Pilate was drawn to a much smaller scale in black chalk than was originally indicated by the incising (pl. 6). Similarly, the two kneeling figures in the foreground were drawn substantially larger in black chalk. Ruled incised lines define the embrasure of the doors, and later, ruled black chalk lines were added parallel to them. A single ruled line in red chalk extends vertically down the center of the sheet, parallel to and beneath the black chalk passages. This is the only deliberate application of red chalk evident anywhere on the sheet.[8] Partial incising of the stairs in the foreground spatially establishes them in the composition. The grouping of figures superimposed over the stairs is clearly a later modification in the composition and one that disrupts its structural unity (pl. 8).

Once Pontormo turned directly to drawing with the stick of black chalk, he proceeded to layer the drawn lines until ultimately almost every passage appears to carry *pentimenti* beneath it. Complicated by the use of stumping throughout, it is difficult to establish the spatial relationships between groupings of figures. Initially, the kneeling figure to the left was much smaller in size and the contours of the form closely followed the incising (pl.

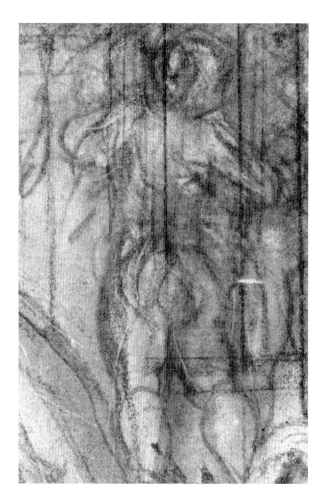

FIGURE 3. Pontormo. *Christ before Pilate* (detail of pl. 1). Photo: Harriet K. Stratis. This detail of the upper right corner of the drawing shows the putto above and to the right of Pilate. Heavily incised lines are clearly legible and establish the outlines of a form that was later modified by the artist in black chalk.

7). The stairs extended much farther to the left of the composition and the doors came down to meet the stairs. A much more open space existed, and a central axis running from the stairs to the top of the doors was established, making Pilate the focal point of the composition. Pontormo then substantially enlarged the kneeling figure, disturbing this axis, and superimposed an enigmatic grouping of figures on the stairs (pl. 8). In so doing, he effectively closed off the space leading to Pilate and shifted more emphasis onto Christ.

As a further step in the process of examining the drawing as thoroughly as possible, infrared reflectography, a technique customarily used to reveal underdrawing in paintings, was used in hopes of deciphering the layered *pentimenti*.[9] Although the infrared reflectogram proves to be nearly as difficult to read as the drawing

FIGURE 4. Raphael Santi (Italian, 1483–1520). *Poetry*, c. 1509. Black chalk, over stylus underdrawing, on laid paper. Windsor Castle, Royal Library. ©Her Majesty Queen Elizabeth II. This drawing exemplifies the technique of using a stylus to create a well-defined underdrawing in which the proportions established by the incising are maintained as the artist proceeds in black chalk.

that the chalk is so evenly dispersed and the individual round particles so finely ground that it is conceivable that the artist applied his medium in powdered form.[12] This handling of the chalk deviates from the more traditional working method of applying the chalk, in stick form, and smudging the chalk strokes with a stump to create a modulated tone. As a powder, the chalk could be applied directly with the blunt end of the stump and worked into the paper fibers. The visual result of this method of application of the dry medium closely approximates that created with an aqueous medium. Gradations of light and dark achieved by evenly distributing the chalk particles over the surface of the cream-toned paper resemble a dilute grey wash.[13]

The use of the underlying paper, set against the darkest passages of stumped shadow, brings a subdued light into the composition. In its present condition, the paper functions as the lightest tone in the composition where it is left bare or in areas where only the most transparent applications of chalk exist. Originally the paper functioned as a middle tone, superseded by white chalk heightening as the lightest tone. Although now virtually invisible to the unaided eye, coarse particles of white chalk are visible under high magnification. Pontormo included heightening in the final stages of drawing and used it sparingly along several folds of drapery. Because these white chalk passages are greatly diminished, it is not possible to formulate a working method for Pontormo's use of this medium in the drawing.[14]

Technical examination of *Christ before Pilate* has allowed a more complete reading of the conceptual and physical evolution of the drawing. It has also helped to establish Pontormo's unconventional use and manipulation of traditional drawing materials to achieve his artistic goals. Pontormo's ability to establish the foundations of a composition, superimpose figures, and rework the design, without completely upsetting the visual continuity of the drawing, attests to the mastery he had over his drawing materials. Volumes were constructed and revised, lines were drawn and redrawn, and the space was modified as the work developed. As these formal changes were motivated by the artist's stylistic intentions, *Christ before Pilate* should be viewed not as an unfinished, unresolved drawing, but rather as a study in which the artist's working method is directly integrated into his evolving concept of the subject.

itself,[10] it nonetheless substantiates visual analysis regarding Pontormo's manipulation of the black chalk medium (fig. 5). The drawn lines, here shown greatly intensified from the gray tones visible in the drawing to the deeper black tones reflected in the infrared image, reveal a vigorous linear application of black chalk to establish and readjust the outlines and contours of forms. Enhanced contrast in the infrared image also improves the legibility of stumped passages. This clearly reveals stumping to be the technique preferred by Pontormo for developing volumetric forms in modulated tones.[11]

The manner in which Pontormo stumped the chalk allowed him to achieve an unusual washlike effect throughout the drawing. Microscopic inspection shows

FIGURE 5. Composite infrared reflectogram of Pontormo's *Christ before Pilate* (pl. 1). Photo: Harriet K. Stratis. The high contrast, composite infrared image enhances details of the drawing by intensifying the drawn and stumped passages of chalk, which makes these passages easier to decipher.

Serendipity in a Solander Box: A Recently Discovered Pastel and Chalk Drawing by Federico Barocci

SUZANNE FOLDS McCULLAGH

Curator of Earlier Prints and Drawings
The Art Institute of Chicago

For many centuries, an artist produced a drawing primarily as a means to an end rather than as an independent work in its own right. A drawing was rarely signed and, unless clearly related to a known work, often became difficult or impossible to attribute or identify when no longer in the hands of the artist. This was particularly true of Italian drawings of the sixteenth and seventeenth centuries, when art academies emphasized drawing in the training of an artist and in the production of a work of art. Indeed, the difficulty of locating and identifying Italian drawings of this period makes clear the importance of a recent discovery in a solander (or storage) box of drawings donated by Katharine Eberley Gurley, the widow of William Frank Eugene Gurley, to the Art Institute (see Foreword). Among the many unmatted drawings in the solander box was a large, colorful chalk and pastel *Christ Child* on greenish-blue laid paper (pl. 4 and fig. 1)—a drawing that, upon further investigation, proved to be a study for the *Virgin and Child with Saint John the Evangelist*, known as the *Madonna di San Giovanni* (fig. 2), by the sixteenth-century Italian painter Federico Barocci (1535–1612).

Federico Barocci's name is not familiar to a wide audience because he chose to work primarily in his small native town of Urbino. He produced relatively few major altarpieces, and he confined his activities to Urbino and other provincial centers. As a result, Barocci's work has become better known and appreciated through his drawings, which are now scattered among museums and private collections around the world. Barocci's extant drawings are great in number (nearly 2,000 sheets) and high in quality, and they testify to the remarkable energy he brought to his paintings.

This energy is evident in the *Christ Child* study, and it attests to the authenticity of the drawing as a work by Barocci. The question that arose, upon seeing the *Christ Child* among the many British works in the Gurley Collection, was whether it might be a seventeenth- or eighteenth-century copy by a British artist such as Sir Peter Lely, Jonathan Richardson the Elder, or Sir Joshua Reynolds of an earlier Italian work.[1] But the astonishing vitality of the *Christ Child*—with its seemingly palpable baby, whose body moves toward the viewer, suggesting rounded, weighty forms in space—argued against the idea that this might be a later copy.

There were other factors that argued in favor of attributing the *Christ Child* to Barocci. The unresolved areas on the bottom of the page suggested it was a working drawing (see pl. 4). Many of Barocci's drawings were studies for altarpieces depicting the Virgin and Child, and Barocci often reworked and rethought his compositions in such studies.[2] With these facts in mind, it was relatively easy to identify the Art Institute *Christ Child* as a study for the *Madonna di San Giovanni*, c. 1565. In comparing the study and the painting, the purpose of the unresolved

FIGURE 1. Federico Barocci (Italian, 1535–1612). *Christ Child: Study for the "Madonna di San Giovanni"* (detail of pl. 4), c. 1565. Black and red chalk, with pastel and stumping, on greenish-blue laid paper; 40.1 x 26.3 cm. The Art Institute of Chicago, Gift of Mrs. William F. E. Gurley (1990.512.1). Barocci used this remarkably animated study as an actual-size cartoon for the altarpiece known as the *Madonna di San Giovanni* (fig. 2). This drawing is notable for its use of pastel, unusual at the time. Barocci was one of the first artists to employ both pastel and chalk in his studies.

53

FIGURE 2. Federico Barocci. *Madonna di San Giovanni*, c. 1565.
Oil on canvas; 151 x 115 cm. Urbino, Galleria Nazionale delle Marche.
Photo: Soprintendenza per i beni artistici e storici delle Marche, Urbino.
Barocci executed the *Madonna di San Giovanni*, one of his earliest
paintings, after recovering from what his biographer reported was a long
illness. Scholars have proposed that Barocci may have been poisoned by
someone jealous of his talent, but his illness may also have been caused
by lead poisoning, which would have severely restricted his ability to
work with oil paints.

passages in the *Christ Child* became clear: the network of lines were quick thoughts or notations (*pentimenti*) for the Virgin's hand below the Christ Child's right foot, executed characteristically in red chalk to suggest the surging vitality of her warm flesh; the fluttering movement of the Virgin's fingers captures her attempt to hold the Child's moving foot.

Executed in black and colored chalk and pastel[3] on paper originally blue but now faded to a greenish blue in color, the *Christ Child* not only represents a characteristic type of drawing and technique for Barocci but, because of its relationship to the early *Madonna di San Giovanni*, appears to be one of the earliest such drawings known. Moreover, as a point-by-point comparison of the study to the painting reveals, Barocci used the *Christ Child* as an actual-size cartoon for the *Madonna di San Giovanni*.[4] Unlike Barocci's later altarpieces, there are relatively few extant studies for the *Madonna di San Giovanni*; those that have survived, however, are evidence of his earliest attempts to use an elaborate method in preparing a painting. Edmund Pillsbury, a noted scholar now working on a complete catalogue of Barocci's drawings, has written the clearest and most comprehensive account of the artist's usual working method:

It would seem that Barocci began his preparations with figure studies from the nude to establish the poses and draperies of the principal figures. These led to a *disegno compito*, or developed compositional sketch, which served as the basis for color and light studies. . .as well as for the full-scale cartoon. After transferring the design of the cartoon to the panel or canvas, normally by means of stylus incisions, the artist laid out the broad outlines of the composition in a rapid monochrome *abbozzo*. At this juncture he turned to large-scale detail studies

. . .to fix the color, the light, or a particular aspect of the composition. . . .Through the use of stylus incisions and a squared grid, he maintained the correct pose and scale of the figures throughout the process. . . .The system, though seeming to be unnecessarily involved and protracted, had a purpose. It provided both flexibility and control, and was ideally suited to the artist's temperament and sense of perfectionism.[5]

The corpus of studies for the *Madonna di San Giovanni*, as the earliest example of Barocci's method, varies slightly from the norm, based on those drawings that are extant. In this case, no nude figure studies are known. It would appear that the first sketches (*primi pensieri*) for the *Madonna di San Giovanni* are those found in the Galleria degli Uffizi (figs. 3–4).[6] On one side, the elements of the composition are broadly indicated—a saint kneels before a Madonna and Child; the Virgin's head is more frontal but the infant's gesture is already clear. On the reverse, a detail of the Madonna and Child specifies the ultimate angle of the Virgin's head and her cradling the infant's foot. However, uncertainty over the infant's gesture is discernible in the various conceptions (*pentimenti*) noted in the sketch. Although executed with just a few strokes of red chalk on an extremely small piece of blue paper, these sketches pinpoint the essential characteristics of the composition, the general outline of the forms, and the emotive quality of the figures.[7]

Unusual among the known studies for the *Madonna di San Giovanni* is a large chalk and pastel *modello* (or finished drawing) in the Scholz Collection documenting the development of the composition at its mid-point (fig. 5). This sheet seems to have come fairly late in the process, probably reflecting the color adjustments made after

FIGURE 3. Federico Barocci. *Study for the "Madonna di San Giovanni,"* c. 1565 (verso). Red chalk on blue paper; 17.2 x 11.7 cm. Florence, Galleria degli Uffizi (11545F). This drawing and the next (fig. 4) are possibly the first studies for the *Madonna di San Giovanni*; rendered here are only the broad outlines of a saint kneeling before the Virgin and Child.

FIGURE 4. Federico Barocci. *Study for the "Madonna di San Giovanni,"* c. 1565 (recto). Red chalk on blue paper; 17.2 x 11.7 cm. Florence, Galleria degli Uffizi (11545F). In this study Barocci sketched with great economy the position of the Virgin and Child as they would later appear in the altarpiece.

FIGURE 5. Federico Barocci. *Virgin and Child with Kneeling Saint John the Evangelist (Madonna di San Giovanni)*, c. 1565. Black, red, and white chalk, with traces of ocher, on blue paper now faded; squared for transfer in red and black chalk; varnished; 48.2 x 40.2 cm. New York, The Pierpont Morgan Library, Janos Scholz Collection. (1978.37) This study is a remnant of a *modello* that Barocci used to paint the *Madonna di San Giovanni*.

the creation of the full-scale cartoon. First published by Pillsbury in *The Graphic Art of Federico Barocci*,[8] this unusual piece was described there as the sort of highly finished *modello* (or cartoon?) which the early seventeenth-century historian G. B. Bellori said the artist used "to investigate the color juxtapositions after making the full-scale model."[9] Although it records the composition as it had developed to that point, *pentimenti* and variations from the final painting testify that the work is procedural, and not a copy.

No monochrome *abbozzo* is known to exist. Also coming at this point in the process, that is after a full-scale cartoon had been drawn and the design transferred to canvas, according to Pillsbury's scheme, were other color studies, such as those he identified for the head of the Virgin (fig. 6) and the figure of Saint John.[10] The former was outlined primarily in black chalk with red chalk accents for the facial features and ocher added for the hair—the predominant materials in the Art Institute's

Christ Child. In addition to this more idealized portrayal of the Virgin's head that Barocci actually utilized, several studies of the same head drawn from life have been identified in the Musée du Louvre, Paris (see fig. 7).[11] These naturalistic studies are either an indication of Barocci's return to life study at this juncture or, as Pillsbury's scheme suggests, the initial studies from the model that inspired Barocci to undertake this composition. So close are the life studies to the idealized cartoon (fig. 6) that it is impossible to determine where they fall in the process.

Within this context, the Art Institute drawing plays an unusual role. No previously identified life studies for the child have survived, but the quality of naturalism in the sheet suggests it was drawn from an actual child. Ostensibly a characteristic "large-scale detail" study used to fix the color and light, the *Christ Child* also seems to have served as a cartoon, as revealed by its point-by-point correspondence with the painting. Because the sheet is not incised with a stylus, it does not fit into Pillsbury's description of Barocci's mature working method and therefore represents the artist's earliest experimentations. Perhaps using the squared Scholz drawing, the artist must have devised another means of transferring the image to the canvas.[12]

To fully appreciate the importance of the discovery of the Art Institute *Christ Child*, we must survey briefly Barocci's early career up to 1565, the approximate date of the *Madonna di San Giovanni*. We will examine the style and technique of the *Christ Child* vis-à-vis Barocci's relationship to other Italian artists, as well as the prominent role of drawings in Barocci's art and his use of pastel and colored chalk techniques. We will see that behind Barocci's choice of media and technique for the *Christ Child* study were personal and medical considerations that figured importantly in the development of the *Madonna di San Giovanni* altarpiece.

Federico Barocci was born around 1535 into an esteemed artisan family of Lombard origin that had for several generations served the court of Urbino — itself the setting of Baldassare Castiglione's renowned book, *The Courtier*.[13] By the early sixteenth century, the stature that Federico da Montefeltro had brought to the court was waning, and the dynasty under his son Guidobaldo was drawing to an end.[14] Yet the cultural prominence of this remote site in the region of the Marches was maintained not only in the decorations of the Ducal Palace and the Cathedral, but more widely in the work of renowned artists who scattered across Italy from Urbino and its environs: the antiquarian Girolamo Genga (1467–1551), the great High Renaissance artist Raphael (1483–1520) and, later, the brothers Taddeo (1529–1566) and Federico (1540/41–1609) Zuccaro, who galvanized mid-century Rome with their decorations and substantial following.

Barocci was the great-grandson of a sculptor named Ambrogio, whose bas reliefs prominently decorated the Ducal Palace. His father and grandfather also specialized in watchmaking and gem-cutting.[15] He undoubtedly

FIGURE 6. Federico Barocci. *Head of a Young Woman Looking to Lower Right*, c. 1565. Black and red chalks, with ocher and stumping, on light beige paper; 24 x 18.8 cm. New York, The Metropolitan Museum of Art, Gustavus A. Pfeiffer Fund (64.136.3). In this idealized color study for the *Madonna di San Giovanni*, Barocci used some of the same materials (black and red chalks and ocher) that dominate the Art Institute *Christ Child* (pl. 4).

FIGURE 7. Federico Barocci. *Study for the "Madonna di San Giovanni,"* c. 1565. Black and red chalk on brownish paper; 27.2 x 20 cm. Paris, Musée du Louvre (inv. 2864). Photo: Andrea Emiliani, *Federico Barocci (Urbino 1535–1612)*, vol. 1 (Bologna, 1985), p. 24. Unlike the idealized *Head of a Woman Looking to Lower Right* (fig. 6), this study appears to have been drawn from life.

received his earliest training from his father at home, but soon came under the influence of the painter Giovanni Battista Franco (c. 1498–1561), who came from Venice to decorate the Cathedral from about 1546 to 1549, *en route* to Rome. Battista Franco was an anomaly in sixteenth-century Italy as an artist who traveled widely and absorbed divergent influences from Venice to Rome. The importance of this formative contact with an established artist from a cultural capital in the north cannot be minimized, as Franco surely imparted to the young Barocci a Venetian bias towards color in both drawing and painting, and may well have shown him examples of contemporary Venetian draftsmanship in colored chalks and pastels on blue paper by such artists as Jacopo Bassano (fig. 8).[16] Barocci's interest in Titian dominated his subsequent apprenticeship from about 1549 to 1553 in Pesaro with his uncle, Bartolommeo Genga (1516–1558), architect to Duke Guidobaldo.

Barocci's first journey to Rome, where he was part of the circle of Taddeo Zuccaro, probably from 1553 to 1555, was "stimulated by the desire for fame and by the name of his countryman, Raphael," to quote Bellori.[17] Taddeo, virtually Barocci's contemporary, had been established there for ten years and is said to have helped his younger colleague to visit and study the masterpieces of antiquity and the High Renaissance, which they copied together, and to participate in major commissions, such as that for the Mattei chapel which Taddeo began in 1553. Raphael was unquestionably an extremely compelling example for Barocci, not only in the majestic naturalism of his figures and proclivity toward Holy Family subjects, but also in the renowned method of preparation developed by Raphael and his workshop. Indeed, Raphael provided the most obvious model for Barocci's elaborate utilization of many different kinds of drawings in preparation for a painting. It is said that Barocci owned some drawings by Raphael,[18] and the intellectual and stylistic burden of Raphael's preeminence must have been tremendous for him.

Moreover, Taddeo Zuccaro seems to have introduced Barocci to even other, more remote currents of recent artistic expression which had filtered to him in the international artistic capital of Rome—notably in the formative art of Correggio (1489/94–1534), whose major paintings were to be found in the north of Italy, in Emilia. How Correggio's art was transmitted to Rome is unclear; whether by prints, drawings, or oil sketches, it incited in the Zuccaro brothers and Barocci an interest in emotion, atmosphere, and luminism, and Barocci was particularly responsive to these influences. It is now believed that the young Barocci may even have journeyed to Parma and Modena in the following years, 1555–60, to experience Correggio's paintings firsthand.[19]

FIGURE 8. Jacopo Bassano (Italian, 1517–1592). *Head of an Apostle.* Charcoal, red chalk, and pastel on blue paper; 13.2 x 13.2 cm. Vienna, Albertina (Inv. 1553; v. 72). Bassano's subtle combination of pastel and chalk in drawings such as *Head of an Apostle* was a likely influence on Barocci's pastel technique.

The lure of his countryman's involvement with major Roman commissions must have drawn Barocci back to Rome in the years 1561–63, when he worked with Zuccaro and other artists on the decoration of the Casino of Pius IV and the Belvedere in the Vatican.[20] Barocci's contribution at this time was substantial and recognized. Just a few years later, in the second edition of his *Lives of the Most Eminent Painters, Sculptors, and Architects* of 1568, Giorgio Vasari referred to Barocci in the "Life of Taddeo Zuccaro" as a "youth of great promise."[21]

Since Barocci's own day, it has been believed that this tremendous promise must have spawned great jealousy. For this reason, Barocci thought he had been poisoned in 1563, and was forced to put down his brushes, abandon his career in Rome, and return dramatically to Urbino. Bellori maintained that, "as the result of the perversity of a few painters, who, incited by jealousy, invited him to a light meal and poisoned his salad... [Barocci] succumbed to such an incurable disease that not only could no remedies be found...before the acute pain subsided, [but] four years transpired during which the artist suffered without ever being able to touch a brush."[22]

His condition has at times been considered the characteristic melancholy of artistic genius, or possibly a form of neurosis or psychosomatic disease; clearly something occurred that completely transformed Barocci's life, making it difficult for him to paint from that day forward, crippling him physically, or psychologically, or both.[23] Bellori further commented on the effects:

It certainly seems incredible to hear of so many public as well as private works having been executed by this master when his incurable illness allowed him only to work for an hour in the morning and another in the evening. Nor could he prolong his effort even in thought, let alone touch a brush or draw a single line. . . . All the rest of the day he spent in pain from stomach cramps, caused by continuous vomiting which overcame him as soon as he had eaten.

At night he hardly slept, and even during that short time he was tormented by frightful dreams, and sometimes he moaned and made so much noise that one person would stay by him and wake him on purpose, in order to free him from this oppression. So it went on ever since the day on which he believed he had been poisoned until his death, that is, for fifty-two years.[24]

Most recently, Barocci's ailment—along with the similar sufferings of many other distinguished artists—has been identified as plumbism, or lead poisoning.[25] This was the same affliction that forced the eighteenth-century French artist Jean Siméon Chardin to relinquish oil paints in his late years, in favor of pastels.[26] The highly toxic nature of most paints and solvents was largely ignored until recently; they undoubtedly affected some highly susceptible artists more severely than others.

It is noteworthy that Barocci began to work in colored chalk and pastels in the mid-1560s, just after the poisoning occurred, as is demonstrated by the recently discovered *Christ Child* in the Art Institute. This work—together with the other less elaborate detail studies for the *Madonna di San Giovanni*—marks the first active cultivation and integration of the pastel and colored chalk technique into normal working methods by an Italian artist.[27] It is also possibly the first known instance of a medical necessity for a natural alternative to coloristic expression, as echoed two centuries later in the portraits of Chardin.

The exact nature of Barocci's work immediately after 1563 is unclear, if he was able to work at all. Bellori related his eventual deliverance:

Lamenting above all the fact that he could not paint, one day he prayed to the heavenly Virgin with such conviction that he was heard. Feeling an improvement in his health, he made a small painting with the Virgin and Christ Child who blesses the young Saint John and presented it as a votive offering to the Capuchin fathers of Crocicchia, two miles outside of Urbino, where he often would stay on a farm of his.[28]

Indeed, Barocci apparently joined the Capuchin order at about the same time that he painted the *Madonna di San Giovanni* (now in the Galleria Nazionale delle Marche, Urbino) in 1566.

It would seem, then, that the painting of the *Madonna di San Giovanni* owes its existence to the remission of Barocci's medical affliction, and the very method of its preparation was possibly determined by that condition. Such an ailment could also have prompted him to plan his oils elaborately with pastel and chalk drawings.[29]

The use of colored chalks and pastels was relatively limited in sixteenth-century Italy. Leonardo is said to have been the first Italian artist to have introduced pastel into his drawings with his portrait of Isabella d'Este of Mantua, 1499 (see, in this issue, Bernardina Sani, "Rosalba Carriera's *Young Lady with a Parrot*," fig. 4); he claimed to have learned the technique from a French artist, Jean Perréal, who visited Milan in 1499 with Louis XII.[30] Few other early examples of pastels can be cited beyond this work. It is not impossible that Barocci might have known Leonardo's famous portrait; its restricted palette—consisting primarily of ocher touches in the hair—parallels the golden coloring of the *Christ Child*. Bellori, however, traced Barocci's technical inspiration to Correggio's example, which he might have encountered shortly before his second voyage to Rome around 1560:

During that period there arrived in Urbino a painter who was returning from Parma with some large sheets [*pezzi di cartoni*] and some exquisite heads drawn in colored chalks [*pastelli*] by Correggio. . .thereafter, he began to draw with colored chalks from life. . . . Barocci profited from the excellent style of Correggio, and imitated it in the gentle expressions of his heads, and in the blending of his tones [*sfumatione*] and the gentleness [*soavità*] of the color.[31]

Whether this incident is true or whether Barocci made a pilgrimage to Emilia to see Correggio's works—as suggested above—the influence of Correggio's coloring, expression, and compositions for Barocci is undeniable. No other artist could have instilled in Barocci such a heightened spirituality combined with diaphanous, golden hues. No large chalk studies are known by Correggio, however, and the possibility that some once existed is mere speculation. The best existing examples of pastel or chalk drawings that could have served as direct inspiration for Barocci emanate from Venice, where the use of blue paper was also promoted. Barocci's Venetian mentor, Battista Franco, could easily have shared with him (or told him of) drawings by artists such as Bassano (fig. 8) combining colored chalks and pastel on colored paper—the most pertinent and plausible source for a technique Barocci eventually cultivated more than any other artist of his century.

The influences of Correggio, Raphael, and other artists are especially evident in other aspects of the *Madonna di San Giovanni* altarpiece. Correggio did establish a notable practice, in the second decade of the sixteenth century, of small-scale altarpieces devoted to the Madonna and Child interacting with the infant Saint John the Baptist (who corresponds to the figure of Saint John the Evangelist in the *Madonna di San Giovanni*). The expressive interaction of Barocci's figures and the landscape backdrop of the *Madonna di San Giovanni* bear comparison to those very works by Correggio — such as the *Virgin and Child with the Young Saint John the Baptist*, c. 1515, in the Art Institute (fig. 9) — which would have been the most portable, and therefore potentially accessible, examples of Correggio's art.[32] The slight *sfumato* (shading) and sweetness of Barocci's *Christ Child* may also owe something to Correggio, as well as the infant's golden locks and the overall palette of the painting.

It is the opinion of this author that the relatively unusual palette of the *Madonna di San Giovanni* —

emphasizing cool blues and forest greens with golden highlights, in contrast to the often hot, acrid hues of Barocci's maturity — owes less to specific influences from Correggio or Lorenzo Lotto[33] than to the introduction of chalk and pastel studies on colored paper. The limited chalks and pastels utilized by Barocci at the outset of his career — including natural red, black, and possibly ocher chalks and some pink pastel, in the case of the *Christ Child* — as well as the critical role of the blue paper background, may have determined the relatively cool tonality of the final painting. Indeed, the colors of the Art Institute study reflect exactly those hues of the oil. This theory — that the colors of the chalks and pastel might have determined the painting's color palette — presents an early deviation from Barocci's later procedure as proposed by Marilyn Lavin, that Barocci eventually chose his colors for drawing specifically in order to study the effect of those hues anticipated in the final painting.[34]

FIGURE 9. Correggio (Antonio Allegri; Italian, c. 1494–1534). *Virgin and Child with the Young Saint John the Baptist*, c. 1515. Oil on panel; 64.2 x 50.2 cm. The Art Institute of Chicago, Clyde M. Carr Collection (1965.688). This painting is one of the finest early works by Correggio in America. The gentle tone and golden palette of a small-scale altarpiece such as this may have influenced Barocci's *Madonna di San Giovanni* (fig. 2).

Compositionally, the ultimate influence for Barocci, both generically and specifically, can be found in the art of Raphael. Raphael was best known for his many Madonna and Child compositions. Two paintings of 1506 that he ostensibly executed in Urbino for Guidobaldo da Montefeltro feature the Madonna cradling her infant's foot—the very motif that is the trademark of the *Madonna di San Giovanni*: *The Orléans Madonna* (fig. 10) and the *Madonna with the Beardless Saint Joseph*.[35] In adopting this motif, Barocci consciously allied himself with his illustrious predecessor.

One of the compelling features of the *Christ Child* study in Chicago is the engaging manner in which the infant reaches out of the picture in contrast to the averted, introspective glance of the Virgin and the devotional pose of John the Evangelist. This image of the active, outreaching *Christ Child* appears frequently in Barocci's work, but rarely with the fresh spontaneity of the Chicago drawing.

For example, in the fresco of the *Holy Family* from the Casino of Pius IV, 1561–63 (fig. 11), the child reaches across his body, closing himself off from the viewer in a posture that contrasts with the child's more vulnerable expression in the Art Institute's drawing.[36] A slightly later composition, the *Madonna di San Simone* (fig. 12), maintains the child's open torso but relaxes it, turning it into a less natural, more mannered and elegant pose, despite its foundation in countless rapid pen sketches of a squirming child.[37] His later evolution of this compositional type can be seen in the *Madonna del Gatto* (fig. 13) and the *Rest on the Flight into Egypt*—the latter made famous in an anonymous woodcut (fig. 14)—depicting a slightly older Christ Child interacting with his mother in a more active and complex way.

It has been noted frequently that Barocci's draftsmanship shows remarkably little development across the course of his career. Despite this assertion, there has remained a need for a more serious study of the artist's

FIGURE 10. Raphael Santi (Italian, 1483–1520). *The Orléans Madonna*, 1506. Oil on panel; 29 x 21 cm. Chantilly, Musée Condé. Raphael's influence on Barocci was more compositional than coloristic. In *The Orléans Madonna*, Raphael used the motif of the Virgin cradling the Christ Child's foot that Barocci later included in the *Madonna di San Giovanni* (fig. 2).

FIGURE 11. Federico Barocci. *The Holy Family*, 1561–63. Fresco. Rome, Vatican, Casino of Pius IV. Barocci's fresco, part of an elaborate vault in a papal villa in the Vatican, portrays the Christ Child in a less open pose than is found in the Art Institute's *Christ Child* (pl. 4).

FIGURE 12. Federico Barocci. *Madonna di San Simone*, c. 1567. Oil on canvas; 283 x 190 cm. Urbino, Galleria Nazionale delle Marche. Photo: Emiliani, *Federico Barocci*, vol. 1, p. 42. This painting and the next two works (figs. 13-14) illustrate the range of expression Barocci imparted to the Virgin and Child theme.

drawings.[38] For an artist who very early turned to many different media, techniques, and styles as he prepared for a painting, it is difficult to note the maturation of Barocci's draftsmanship simultaneously in all arenas. Nonetheless, in the studies for the *Madonna di San Giovanni*, the artist's tentative beginnings can be observed in the *Christ Child*, in the problematic foreshortening of the infant's left arm and right leg, and in the relative flatness of his chest and shoulder area. The preponderance of rich, black chalk outlines and regular hatching marks an early stage in the integration of color in the artist's technique; a similar reliance on black chalk is found in a *Head of a*

Young Woman Looking to Lower Right (fig. 6), which is largely executed in black and red chalks with only touches of ocher and pink pastel.

In later years, color would dominate in finished head studies such as the *Head of the Virgin* (fig. 15) for the *Annunciation* (Vatican Museum, Rome) of 1582/84. For this reason, comparison with a drawing in the Cleveland Museum of Art of a *Seated Angel Preparing to Shoot a Bow and Arrow*, which is heavily heightened with pastels of many shades, strengthens the argument that the latter is more likely by "a studio assistant or close follower rather than by Barocci himself."[39] Although shortcom-

FIGURE 13. Federico Barocci. *Madonna del Gatto*, 1573/74. Oil on canvas; 112.7 x 92.7 cm. London, National Gallery. Reproduced by courtesy of the Trustees, the National Gallery, London.

FIGURE 14. After Federico Barocci. *Rest on the Flight into Egypt.* Chiaroscuro woodcut; 34.8 x 28.1 cm. The Art Institute of Chicago, Gift of Frank B. Hubachek in memory of Alfred E. Hamill (1968.298).

FIGURE 15. Federico Barocci. *Head of the Virgin*, 1582/84. Black, white, and colored chalk on blue-gray paper; 29.9 x 23 cm. Windsor Castle, Royal Library (inv. 5231). ©1991 Her Majesty Queen Elizabeth II. In this study for the *Annunciation* (Vatican Museum, Rome) of 1582/84, Barocci used pastel sparingly to create a very natural, polished drawing of the Virgin.

FIGURE 16. Federico Barocci. *Figure Studies*, c. 1566. Black and white chalk, with stumping, contours (of large study) incised, on light blue paper; 39.4 x 27 cm. Washington, D. C., National Gallery of Art, Ailsa Mellon Bruce Fund (1983.17.1). By permission of the National Gallery of Art.

ings in the modeling and awkwardness of line of the *Seated Angel* have prompted analogies with the *Madonna di San Giovanni* studies prior to the discovery of the Art Institute *Christ Child*,[40] the relative yet compelling reserve of the latter point up the superficiality of the *Seated Angel*. The broader *sfumato* effects characteristic of later, more polished head studies, such as that in Windsor (fig. 15), result less from the quantity of color or pastel than from the selective use of it. The natural quality of the *Christ Child* is principally a product of this restrained technique, whereas the *Seated Angel* in Cleveland has an aura of sugary fantasy in its reliance on pastels to create a definable presence.

The Art Institute's study stands out as a work at once complete and painterly, fragmentary and graphic. It achieves the former in its balanced and integrated colorism, with the black and colored chalks playing off the tinted paper; yet the artist's hand is evident in the transitional and graphic quality of its broad chalk handling and

pentimenti. Satisfying as an independent composition, it nonetheless reflects its relationship to a thoroughly conceived compositional whole in the gaze and gesture of the child and the hint of the Virgin's hand.[41] It stands in marked contrast in conception to the other preparatory stages of Barocci's drawings, such as the more schematic nude figure studies (fig. 16) for the *Crucifixion with the Mourning Virgin and Saint John*, which otherwise relate closely in handling.[42]

Nearly two centuries in advance of the full flowering of pastel under artists such as Rosalba Carriera, Barocci established the authority of pastel — even when used in a preparatory work — as an independent drawing in its own right, by the scale, placement, and finish of the *Christ Child* study. This is made all the more clear when this work is compared to the fragmentary monochrome cartoon *Head of the Virgin*, also in Chicago (fig. 17), which was irregularly cut and incised with a stylus as an actual preparatory scaffold for the *Deposition* in the Cathedral, Perugia, of 1567/69.[43] The survival of this fragment of the cartoon is totally coincidental; rough sketches on the back indicate it was a working sheet trimmed for expediency of transfer, with no regard to aesthetics. The *Christ Child*, by contrast, is not only centered on its fine blue paper, it bears no other studies on the back. It seems thus less a working drawing than a work of art in its own right, equivalent to a small painting, as pastels would be regarded in later centuries.

Poised on the cusp of the Renaissance and the Baroque, Barocci played a pivotal role in the development of pastel and the emancipation of drawing as an independent art form. The discovery of the *Christ Child* in Chicago offers an important key to this overall picture and to the complex working method of Barocci in particular.

FIGURE 17. Federico Barocci. *Head of the Virgin*, 1568/69. Black chalk and charcoal, with stumping and traces of white chalk, on tan laid paper, pieced and incised; max. 29.4 x 23.9 cm. The Art Institute of Chicago, Leonora Hall Gurley Memorial Collection (1922.5406). This fragmentary cartoon has an unfinished quality that contrasts with the careful execution of the *Christ Child* (pl. 4). The irregular cutting and tracing of this cartoon shows that Barocci used it strictly as a means to an end, and was not thinking of it as an independent work of art.

Giovanni Benedetto Castiglione's *God Creating Adam*: The First Masterpiece in the Monotype Medium

SUE WELSH REED

Museum of Fine Arts, Boston

Many artists have been stimulated by their first sight of an inventive monotype and have been inspired to try their hand at this unique image-making process.[1] Giovanni Benedetto Castiglione (1609–1664), an Italian painter and etcher from Genoa, was almost certainly the inventor of this improvisational technique. *God Creating Adam* (pl. 3 and fig. 1) may well have been one of the first monotypes he pulled from the press almost 350 years ago. In a perfect match of technique and subject, the artist used his newly invented printmaking method to portray the central scene of creation, an image that pulsates with light and energy. The Art Institute of Chicago is extremely fortunate in having been able to acquire this important work of art, formerly part of the preeminent collection of the Duke of Devonshire at Chatsworth, for it is among Castiglione's most powerful monotypes and one of only three examples of his work in this medium in the United States.[2]

The art of making monotypes is the province of painters and etchers, especially those who value spontaneity and can see the expressive possibilities in an accidental effect, a wayward brushstroke, or an untidy line caused when the acid bit the plate improperly. Castiglione used the simplest and most direct means to make *God Creating Adam*. He took a polished copper plate, such as would have been prepared for the use of an etcher or engraver, and coated it evenly with a layer of viscous black printing ink. He drew his design on the inked plate, using a stick or the handle of a paintbrush. As he drew, the ink was pushed aside or removed from the smooth surface. When the completed plate and a sheet of dampened printing paper were run through the rolling-bed press, the inky image was transferred to the paper in the form of white lines on a black background. This method is usually called "dark ground," to distinguish it from the monotypes Castiglione created by painting a positive image with brush and oily pigment on a plate that was printed with an uninked background.

When *God Creating Adam* was made about 1645, the intaglio printmaking methods of engraving and etching already had a long tradition. Engraving first came into use in the mid-fifteenth century, while etching made its appearance as a printmaking medium in the early sixteenth century. But it

FIGURE 1. Giovanni Benedetto Castiglione (Italian, 1609–1664). *God Creating Adam* (detail of pl. 3), c. 1645. Monotype in black ink on ivory laid paper (dark-ground manner); 30.2 x 20.5 cm. The Art Institute of Chicago, Restricted gift of Dr. and Mrs. William D. Shorey and promised gift of an anonymous donor (1985.1113). Castiglione was almost certainly the inventor of the monotype, and *God Creating Adam* may have been one of the first monotypes he printed. The artist created this monotype by coating a polished copper plate with black ink, drawing on the inked plate with a stick or paintbrush handle, and then printing the image on a sheet of paper.

was not until the seventeenth century that changes in the artistic climate provided the opportunity for the invention of monotype. Among these changes was a growing appreciation of the suggestive rather than the defined image. Drawings, formerly considered means to an end, were now collected and treasured as independent works of art. Painters such as Peter Paul Rubens favored oil sketches to work out their compositions. Artists of the Baroque period were able to choose from a range of styles, and they used media and techniques in a less orthodox manner than artists of the Renaissance. Castiglione was among the more technically explorative artists of his time, seeking to reproduce the tonal qualities of painting in his drawings and prints, and it is not surprising that he was the creator of the monotype process.[3]

Castiglione was baptized on March 23, 1609, in Genoa, where he trained under minor painters who specialized in landscapes and animals. He became familiar with works by Flemish and Venetian painters that were warmly colored and lushly executed. Throughout his career, animals played a large role in his work, and he often returned to themes such as Noah and the animals, shepherds and their flocks, and pagan pastorals and sacrifices. With his restless personality, Castiglione has been aptly characterized by Mary Newcome as "a constant, irrepressible traveler," who, like the herds of animals he portrayed, was constantly on the move. Although he always maintained contact with his native city, he worked in Rome and Naples in the

FIGURE 2. Giovanni Benedetto Castiglione. *A Pagan Sacrifice*, late 1640s. Oil paint on tan laid paper, laid down on cream wove paper; 57.6 x 42.5 cm. The Art Institute of Chicago, Clarence Buckingham Collection (1968.77). Castiglione is known to have worked in many media, and this drawing exhibits the spontaneous effects he could achieve on paper with a brush and various oil paints.

FIGURE 3. Giovanni Benedetto Castiglione. *Pastoral Journey with a Youth on a Pony*, 1638. Etching; 19.8 x 25 cm. Collection of the Wellesley College Museum, Museum Purchase (1984.30).

FIGURE 4. Michelangelo Buonarotti (Italian, 1475–1564). *The Creation of Adam*, c. 1511. Fresco on the ceiling of the Sistine Chapel, Rome. Castiglione possibly created his monotype of the creation scene in response to Michelangelo's *Creation of Adam*, which Castiglione would have been able to see when he was in Rome in the 1630s and 1640s.

1630s and 1640s and later in Venice and Mantua, where he died in 1664.[4] He may also have spent time in Florence, Parma, Bologna, and Modena. From 1645 to 1647, Castiglione returned to Genoa, where he executed a number of important church altarpieces and painted and drew pagan and pastoral subjects for private collectors. During this period he made a number of etchings and related monotypes.

Castiglione's artistic personality seemed perfectly suited to the invention of monotype. The artist often began his canvases with a dark background and built up his image with light, bright colors. He drew with pen, ink, and wash in a traditional manner, but he also executed many unusual experimental sheets employing brush and oil pigments in a spontaneous manner. He used brown or red-brown paint, both in combination, and sometimes incorporated shades of red, blue, green, white, and yellow.[5] A superb example of such a drawing is his *Pagan Sacrifice* (fig. 2), also in the collections of The Art Institute of Chicago. When Castiglione made prints, he often experimented to achieve atmospheric and tonal effects, and he pushed the etching process to its limits, accepting the blotches and imperfections that appeared in the final prints. An example is *Pastoral Journey with a Youth on a Pony* (fig. 3), an early etching dated 1638, which, despite its uneven biting and streaked, patchy appearance, makes a satisfying artistic statement.[6] The soft, indefinite quality of line finds its equivalent in the artist's brush drawings. Throughout his work, regardless of the media he chose, Castiglione attempted to create broad tonal effects of light and shadow.

Most of Castiglione's dark-ground monotypes depict nocturnal scenes, illuminated rationally by torchlight or mystically by heavenly radiance.[7] In *God Creating Adam*, the artist evokes the primordial darkness of earth into which God brought light. The scene is the sixth day, on which God created all living creatures, animals and mankind. White lines along the horizon suggest both the rising dawn and the division of earth and water from the heavens. Broad, angular strokes of white were used to extract the half-length figure of God emerging from a cloud, his halo shooting forth lightninglike beams of light. The light emanating from him illuminates the scene below. A spit of barren ground provides the base for the tree-trunk-shaped lump of matter that helps to support the languid body of Adam, bearded in the image of his Maker. The first man's supple body was extricated out of the black ink with abundant, finely drawn lines.

While he frequently repeated certain themes, especially those with pastoral overtones, Castiglione depicted the subject of God creating Adam only once—in this monotype.[8] Several antecedents contribute to a better understanding of the context of the image. While the first account of creation provides little visual information—"God created man in his own image" (Genesis 1:27)—the second account offers a more specific image: "And the Lord God formed man of the dust of the ground, and breathed into his nostrils a breath of life; and man became a living soul" (Genesis 2:7). In the sixteenth and early seventeenth centuries, the more common pictorial depiction of the creation of Adam (often combined with the creation of Eve) showed the full-length figure of God standing near a large tree in a landscape that sometimes included animals. Raphael's frequently copied version in the Vatican loggia exemplifies this type. In a far different and highly original version, Michelangelo depicted the act on the ceiling of the Sistine Chapel in Rome (fig. 4). His God is supported in the air, his cloak billowing about him. Castiglione would have been able to see this Renaissance masterpiece when he was in Rome in the 1630s and early 1640s, and it is tempting to view his monotype to some degree as a response to the Sistine version. There are significant differences, however, between the two works. Michelangelo's muscular Adam, though reclining, is conscious and alert, and he reaches out his hand to cooperate with his Maker. Castiglione's passive Adam is the antithesis of Michelangelo's; he makes no effort but only stretches languidly as God touches him on the shoulder to bring him to life. This man of clay, as yet unawakened, derives from a far older tradition.

As with so many biblical themes, Christian art derived the basis of its

FIGURE 5. Parmigianino (Girolamo Francesco Maria Mazzola; Italian, 1503–1540). *Prometheus Animating Man*, 1524/27. Pen, brown ink, and brown wash over black chalk; 13.7 x 15.4 cm. New York, The Pierpont Morgan Library (IV, 45). Castiglione's image of Adam is similar to Parmigianino's vision of the first man—in both works, the newly created being is not yet fully animate or conscious. The similarities between Parmigianino's drawing and Castiglione's monotype show that Castiglione was influenced by pagan portrayals of the creation of man.

imagery for the creation of Adam from pagan depictions of the myth of the Titan Prometheus creating the first man.[9] In the three-part myth, man was first formed, then infused with life, and lastly given a soul. In the carved Roman funerary sarcophagi that illustrate the myth, Prometheus is shown as a muscular, semiclad sculptor who displays his human figure fashioned out of clay or stone, sometimes seen reclining and full scale but more often standing upright on a pedestal as if he were a diminutive statue. In a second scene, a winged genius touches the body with fire to bring it to life, while in the third episode Minerva provides the soul (anima) in the shape of a butterfly or bee. By contrast, Christian teachings promoted the image of a single and simultaneous act of creation by the Trinity—Father, Son, and Holy Spirit. This visually awkward scene, requiring the three figures representing God to be crowded around the figure of man, was rarely depicted on Christian sarcophagi.[10] During the Middle Ages, Prometheus took on the visual aspects of an elderly, robed scholar-magician, and he was sometimes depicted as sharing the role of creator with the Christian God, in a fusion of the pagan and Christian versions of the story. A drawing made between 1524 and 1527 by the brilliant north Italian painter Parmigianino depicts the myth of the creation of man by Prometheus (fig. 5). With one hand the Titan reaches towards the chariot of the sun to signify his theft of fire from the gods, while the other hand helps support the stiff, puppetlike man he has just formed. While it is unlikely that Castiglione actually saw this drawing, the implications that it carries for the Prometheus myth as a source for his monotype are evident. The creation of man, as well as other episodes from the mythological story of Prometheus, continued to be popular allegorical subjects in seventeenth-century Italy. Castiglione's biblical subject participates in the long history of connections with the pagan version of creation.

In seeking visual precedents for the conception and execution of *God Creating Adam*, it seems possible, though not generally discussed, that inspiration came not from painting, but from sculpture. In the mythological representations, the creator—Prometheus—is clearly identified as a sculptor. In making his monotype, Castiglione may have thought of himself in part as a sculptor. He extracted his image out of black ink, not unlike a sculptor gradually producing a figure from a lump of clay or a block of stone. The fine parallel lines defining Adam's body imitate the strokes of a modeling tool or a fine-toothed chisel, while the "tree trunk" echoes the extraneous supports that were necessary appendages to marble sculptures from antiquity to modern times. Works by Castiglione's Roman contemporary Gianlorenzo Bernini could have been a source. Bernini's *Apollo and Daphne* (1622/24), for example, shows the nymph in the midst of metamorphosing into a laurel, her figure inseparable from the marble tree. In such masterpieces Bernini incorporated surface treatment and effects of light almost as if he were painting with marble. An even more interesting comparison can be made between Castiglione's Adam and the *Slaves* (or *Prisoners*) that Michelangelo carved for the tomb of Pope Julius II in St. Peter's, Rome, but which were never installed on the much reduced final monument. Two nearly completed *Slaves* were sent to France in the mid-sixteenth century (they are now in the Musée du Louvre, Paris), and four partially cut blocks remained in Florence. Towards the end of the sixteenth century, they were set up in the Boboli Gardens, where they could be seen for the next three centuries (they are now in the Accademia di Belle Arti). These extraordinary figures apparently struggling to free themselves from the surrounding marble captured the imagination of all observers.[11] Whether he knew the originals, drawings of them, or derivations, Castiglione seems to have had Michel-

FIGURE 6. Michelangelo Buonarotti. *The Awakening Slave*, 1520s. Marble; h. 270.5 cm. Florence, Accademia di Belle Arti. Photo: Florence, Gabinetto Fotografico, Soprintendenza Beni Artistici e Storici. Since the sixteenth century, the contorted poses of Michelangelo's *Slaves* have made an indelible impression on visitors to the Boboli Gardens in Florence, and on numerous others who encountered them through prints and reproductions. Castiglione's monotype — with its image of a twisting Adam being brought to life — seems to have been influenced by Michelangelo's slave struggling to free himself from the surrounding marble.

angelo's sculptures in mind. Adam's twisting pose, one arm flung behind his head, recalls most clearly one of the statues sent to France, although it is not far removed from one of the most remarkably beautiful of those remaining in Florence, aptly entitled *The Awakening Slave* (fig. 6).[12] As the partially completed slave is bound to the block of marble, so the unfinished Adam remains bonded to his genetic lump of clay.

Although he derived elements from mythological imagery and from sculptural poses by Michelangelo, in *God Creating Adam* Castiglione fashioned a unique and electrifying image of his own. With each extractive stroke of his tool, he revealed the process of image making. By bringing light out of darkness, the artist, like his Creator, brought form out of chaos. In an unsurpassed marriage of message and medium, the artist chose to use his newly created art of monotype to depict the most central act of Genesis, the creation of man.

Rosalba Carriera's *Young Lady with a Parrot*

BERNARDINA SANI

Università di Siena

Recently, The Art Institute of Chicago was fortunate to acquire a major pastel, *Young Lady with a Parrot* (front cover, pl. 5, and fig. 1) by Rosalba Carriera, Europe's most famous female painter during the first half of the eighteenth century (fig. 2).[1] Her miniature portraits and pastels were highly regarded in Italy, England, France, and Germany. Born in Venice in 1675, she was the daughter of Andrea Carriera, a Venetian government employee, and Angela Foresti, an embroiderer. There is no documented information on her early training; some sources mention that she learned painting from Giuseppe Diamantini, others from the miniature painter Felice Ramelli. It is clear that, from 1700 on, she was in contact with many Venetian and foreign painters and with collectors who fostered her career. Her sister Angela's marriage to the Venetian painter Antonio Pellegrini testifies to the relations between the Carriera family and artistic circles, as do some of Rosalba's letters referring to artists such as Balestra, Bombelli, Crespi, and Luti.

Through the efforts of Christian Cole, secretary to Lord Manchester, English ambassador to Venice, Rosalba achieved her first official success with her nomination to the Accademia di S. Luca in Rome in 1705. During this early period, she worked mainly as a miniaturist. The degree to which she achieved international fame in this area was acknowledged in an invitation she received from Johann Wilhelm Pfalz, Elector of the Palatinate, to become court miniature painter in Düsseldorf. Rosalba declined the offer but continued to work for various German electors, among them Frederick Augustus II of Saxony, who became the main collector of her works. In his residence in Dresden, he created the so-called Gabinetto di Rosalba, in which he gathered the largest collection in existence of the artist's pastels. Augustus III of Poland sat for a portrait by Rosalba during a trip to Italy in 1713, when he was still crown prince of Saxony, and he continued to collect works by the artist for the rest of his life.

As a result of trips to Italy by important French connoisseurs and collectors such as Pierre Crozat and Pierre Jean Mariette and the painter Nicolas Vleughels, Rosalba Carriera was acclaimed by the French nobility, many of whom commissioned from her pastel portraits, which became the dominant and most significant part of her production. The French artists with whom she began to interact included Antoine Watteau, who honored her with a request for one of her works. She was celebrated in a way that no other female painter had ever experienced: in 1720, she was nominated to the academies of Bologna and Paris, an exceptional honor for any artist, especially so a woman. As a guest of Crozat, she traveled to Paris in March 1720 with her widowed mother, the Pellegrinis, and her sister Giovanna, who served as her assistant. She stayed in Paris until 1721, associating with the best-known French artists—among them Nicolas de Largillière, François de Troy, and Watteau—and depicting in dozens of pastels members of the court, as well as the young king, Louis XV (fig. 3).[2]

FIGURE 1. Rosalba Carriera (Italian; 1675–1757). *Young Lady with a Parrot* (detail of pl. 5), c. 1730. Pastel on blue laid paper; 59.8 x 50 cm. The Art Institute of Chicago, Helen Regenstein Collection (1985.43). Rosalba Carriera, the early eighteenth century's most famous woman artist, established her fame with her pastels, a medium she elevated to high art. This fine example, combining the two major aspects of her work—portraiture and allegory—illustrates well her spirited technique and elegant color sense.

FIGURE 2. Rosalba Carriera. *Self-Portrait*, 1708/1709. Pastel on paper; 71 x 57 cm. Florence, Galleria degli Uffizi. Rosalba's powers of observation and sensitivity to character are particularly evident in this self-portrait, which is compelling for its honesty and lack of artifice.

Upon her return to Venice, Rosalba continued to work as a portraitist, especially for English nobles who, having completed their education with a Grand Tour of Italy, turned to her to immortalize the event by means of a portrait. She made many images for the English merchant and collector Joseph Smith (he became English consul to Venice in 1735), who gathered an imposing collection of the artist's works which later became part of the English royal collections. Commissioned to do portraits of three daughters of the house of Este, Rosalba went to Modena in 1723, where she was able to admire the paintings of Correggio. As her work demonstrates, she was particularly impressed by the sweetness of his madonnas' faces, by the grace of his figures, and by his delicate shading (*sfumato*) of clothing and landscape. Seven years later, in 1730, she traveled abroad for the last time, to Vienna, where she did the portrait of Empress Amalia (Dresden, Gemäldegalerie). Despite her failing eyesight and despondency at the loss through death of

those dearest to her, especially her sister Giovanna in 1737, Rosalba continued to produce refined and expressive pastel portraits. She died in 1757 and is buried in the Venetian church of SS. Vito e Modesto.[3]

Brief History of the Pastel Medium

Rosalba Carriera's fame today is based more on an appreciation of the extraordinary elegance and delicacy of her portraits than on the critical role she played in the development of pastel portraiture as an autonomous genre. This genre, halfway between drawing and painting, reached its maturity in the eighteenth century after several centuries of evolution.[4]

It is not possible here to trace every phase of the evolution of pastel painting; it is sufficient to recall a few examples from the late fifteenth, sixteenth, and seventeenth centuries to illustrate its various uses and purposes and to explain the distinction and modernity of Rosalba's work in pastel with respect to that of her contemporaries.

Up to the eighteenth century, artists used pastel to give shape to an initial idea, to sketch in the heads in preparatory drawings, or to do portraits of a very intimate and private nature. The first known drawings with touches of pastel date from the late Renaissance. We find them, for example, in Leonardo's circle, where, in accordance with this master's aesthetic, pastels served to achieve shading (*sfumature*) of marvelous delicacy: the portrait of Isabella d'Este by Leonardo in the Musée du Louvre, Paris (fig. 4), testifies, in its extraordinary beauty, to the way in which the colored medium of pastel, in this case yellow, adds an almost imperceptible *sfumato* to the preparatory drawing.

In the sixteenth and seventeenth centuries, the role of pastel in the creation of drawings became more evident; this colored medium was no longer used only for finishing touches, but was employed to fill in larger areas contained within the contours, until, toward the end of the seventeenth century, it hid the drawing almost entirely. Thus was born the type of painting we now call pastel.

The portrait painter Ottavio Leoni, who depicted members of Roman society during the first thirty years of the seventeenth century using the three-chalk technique (red, black, and white chalks), demonstrated how pastel could be introduced into a drawing through outlines in very light contours as a simple means of highlighting, as well as an element of physical characterization (see fig. 5). While he often followed Mannerist models and based his likenesses on formulas established for official portraits (for example, emphasizing the sitters' posture and nobility of appearance rather than their features), Leoni in many cases used pastel to achieve a truly new kind of realism, stimulated by his contacts with Caravaggesque circles.[5]

FIGURE 3. Rosalba Carriera. *Portrait of Louis XV as a Young Boy*, c. 1720. Pastel on paper; 45.7 x 35.6 cm. Boston, Museum of Fine Arts. Celebrated as no other female painter before her, Rosalba often portrayed members of European royalty. She executed this sensitive portrait of the young French king during a triumphant visit to Paris, where she was fêted by high society and received into the French Académie, a singular honor for a woman.

FIGURE 4. Leonardo da Vinci (Italian, 1452–1519). *Portrait of Isabella d'Este*, 1499. Black and red chalk and pastel on board; 60 x 46 cm. Paris, Musée du Louvre, Cabinet des Dessins. Photo: Geneviève Monnier, *Pastels: From the 16th to the 20th Century* (New York, 1984), p. 12. Until the eighteenth century, artists used pastel to give shape to an initial idea, to outline the heads in preparatory drawings, or to do intimate portraits. Leonardo was among the earliest practitioners of pastel. In this famous drawing, he used the medium sparingly as heightening in the neckline and the cascade of hair.

A very different example is offered in the work of Federico Barocci. The drawings in which he used pastel (see pl. 4) can be so finished that they resemble his paintings, for which they were often figure studies. He invested them with the magic of his refined coloration and of bizarre color juxtapositions, harmonies, and shadows. Using pastel, Barocci attempted evanescent effects that were very advanced in their approach.[6] In Italy, various painters such as Guido Reni experimented with pastel, but no one reached the point of executing pastel portraits as an independent art form. On the other hand, in France, the painters Robert Nanteuil and Joseph Vivien created an influential type of pastel portrait (see fig. 6). While their consistent use of frontal postures and dignified costumes emphasizes the sitter's rank, underscored by a primarily dark color palette, a certain painterliness in Nanteuil's and Vivien's execution foreshadows the pastel portraits of subsequent decades that would become less severe and then almost frivolous in character.

At the end of the seventeenth century and during the first years of the eighteenth, artists hesitated to let go of the conventions of official portraiture. Painters such as Benedetto Luti alternated between producing head studies in which heavy lines often sharply enclose the colored medium and portraits rich in color and delicate shading (see fig. 7).[7] Such ambivalence can be seen in Rosalba Carriera's first works (see fig. 8),[8] done when the painter had not yet fully mastered the pastel technique. No such uncertainty is to be found in her mature work nor in the work of her students Marianna Carlevaris and Felicita Sartori or of later Italian artists, such as Francesco Pavona and Lorenzo Tiepolo (son of Giambattista), who devoted themselves to this medium. Thus, in Italy, the period in which pastel established itself as an autonomous genre and reached its greatest flowering was the eighteenth century, from the beginnings of Rococo to Neoclassicism. It was then that pastel portraits became fashionable and were highly appreciated by the upper classes. Pastel portraits also tended to assume an international character, avoiding the idiosyncrasies associated with each of the various Italian schools: Venetian colorism, Bolognese classicism, and so forth.

The artists who painted pastel portraits were principally Venetian and all, from Rosalba to Pietro Rotari, from Pavona to Lorenzo Tiepolo, worked for a clientele connected with the courts of Dresden, London, Madrid, Paris, and St. Petersburg. The preference of European high society for this new type of painting is understandable in view of the fact that it was easily adapted to the customs of the time: with this medium, artists were capable of creating images that were realistic and at the same time subtly illusory, presenting an embellished reality, made up and powdered like the faces of the sitters.

FIGURE 5. Ottavio Leoni (Italian, 1587–1630). *Portrait of a Man and a Woman*, 1607. Pencil, chalk, and pastel on paper; 43.2 x 36.2 cm. Genoa, Museo di Palazzo Rosso. Under the influence of the revolutionary realist painter Michelangelo da Caravaggio, Leoni, a Roman portrait painter, often used pastel to achieve a sense of directness and immediacy.

FIGURE 6. Joseph Vivien (French, 1657–1734). *Portrait of an Artist*, 1698. Pastel on paper; 89 x 71.6 cm. Paris, Musée du Louvre, Cabinet des Dessins. Vivien took the pastel medium from an intermediary status to an independent art form. His stately portraits in the technique earned him membership in the Académie as a "pastel painter."

FIGURE 7. Benedetto Luti (Italian, 1666–1724). *Head of a Bearded Man*, 1715. Pastel mounted on board; 32.2 x 26.4 cm. Washington, D.C., National Gallery of Art, Julius S. Held Collection, Ailsa Mellon Bruce Fund. While artists like Luti were capable of producing skillfully shaded, lively pastels such as this portrait head, they did not achieve the velvety and evanescent passages that are hallmarks of Rosalba's style.

Pastel portraits were appreciated because this painterly technique easily lent itself to the realization of the artist's idea and permitted the creation of a type of painting based on touch and delicate shading, capable of evoking at once the sensual and diaphanous forms typical of the Rococo.

The pastel technique is much simpler than oil painting, because it does not always require preparatory drawing or underpainting and almost never any finish. The lightness of the support, generally paper, permitted the works to be transported at minimal expense. Moreover, the modest dimensions of pastel portraits suited an age in which small and refined objects were coveted as much as works of monumental size. The very adaptability of the medium encouraged imitation, so that patrons were easily satisfied with a copy, or with a slightly modified replica, of a portrait that was not of the highest quality in the first place. This prompted the proliferation of poor pastels often passing as the work of good artists.

Rosalba Carriera can be credited as having been the first to give the pastel medium its fullest expression,

to the point that it became one of the fundamental types of Rococo art. Rosalba lived at a time when the Republic of Venice, in slow and steady decline, was witnessing a new flowering in the figurative arts, thanks to artists working in a Rococo style. This renewal was made by contact with the most vital European cultures; Rosalba, like the Venetian artists Ricci and Pellegrini before her and Canaletto and Bellotto afterward, entrusted her artistic growth to continuous relations with international circles.

The results of Rosalba's relations with foreign artists and connoisseurs are noticeable first of all in the dissemination of her works, since her foreign commissions seem to have outnumbered her Italian ones. While the total lack of heroic tone in her portraits and of all rhetoric in her allegories make her pastels much more modern in their approach than that of French artists working in this medium in the first decades of the century, her art nevertheless owes much to French painters, from Largillière to Watteau.[9] Her contact with the oeuvre of Largillière influenced her emphasis on the representation of jewelry, flowers, and animals, all of which increasingly became emblems of luxury and refinement in her images. Watteau's art is fundamental in understanding Rosalba's persistent study of expression, as she strove to render joy, sadness, serenity, dissipation, and so forth.

The bulk of Rosalba's work in pastel can be divided into two categories: specific portraits (mostly female) and allegories. A shrewd judge of character, Rosalba may have enhanced but never obscured the nature of her sitters. Her technique was quite innovative, combining wet and dry methods. She was the first to soften figures with extensive stumping and evolved a virtuoso "dry-brush" pastel technique by dragging the flat side of her chalk lightly over a contrasting color to suggest diaphanous materials. Such details as floral bouquets, lace, and jewelry were often rendered as crisp, wet-chalk accents. Within her "fancy" pieces, she occasionally introduced décolleté poses to add a piquant flavor of mystery and eroticism that anticipates later developments in French art. Indeed, she has been credited with initiating the taste for grace and seduction that characterizes Rococo art at its most evocative.[10]

The Art Institute's Pastel

In *Young Lady with a Parrot*, we see a young female with reddish (or auburn) hair decorated with flowers, ribbons, and jewels, turned in a three-quarter view and holding a parrot with feathers whose color matches perfectly the blue of her dress. With his beak, the parrot pulls the lace on the young woman's blouse, revealing her pure white breast, a motif found as well in several pastels and a miniature (fig. 9) by Rosalba.[11] The vaporous and diaphanous beauty of the pastel medium is striking in the Chicago work, where realism of expression seems to have been less important than the harmony of the colors.

The pastel in Chicago accords perfectly with Rococo taste, in its graceful forms, in its delicate coloring, in the splendor and fragility of the pastel medium, and, finally, in the ambiguity of a theme that, as will be seen below, may have hidden meaning. The originality of the technique—Rosalba's application of the colors not with a brush but directly, with the pastel crayon and with her fingers—is one of the factors that differentiates this work and others by Rosalba from those of the most representative painters in Venice, such as Pellegrini, Giambattista Pittoni, and Sebastiano Ricci, and underscores the great stylistic range of the Rococo.

These qualities are typical of Rosalba's art at its best and allow us not only to attribute the work to her but also to consider it one of her most successful. *Young Lady with a Parrot* shows some affinity with such mature works by Rosalba as the *Portrait of Barbarina Campani* (fig. 10),[12] which would lead us to date it toward the end

FIGURE 8. Rosalba Carriera. *Bacchante Playing a Cymbol*, c. 1712. Pastel on board; 59.2 x 53.3 cm. Munich, Bayerisches Nationalmuseum. The somewhat hesitant execution and awkward passages of this early work indicate Rosalba's struggle to master the pastel medium.

FIGURE 9. Rosalba Carriera. *Girl with a Parrot.* Tempera on ivory; 8.8 x 6.5 cm. Location unknown. The presence of a parrot in several images of women by Rosalba may simply reflect the eighteenth century's attraction to small, exotic animals. The menagerie in Rosalba's oeuvre includes a variety of birds, as well as cats, dogs, and monkeys. But the images may contain poetic resonances as well.

FIGURE 10. Rosalba Carriera. *Portrait of Barbarina Campani,* c. 1730. Pastel on paper; 56.5 x 46.5 cm. Dresden, Gemäldegalerie. The assurance and ambitiousness of this exquisite pastel, a mature work, also characterize the Art Institute's *Young Lady with a Parrot* (pl. 5), which therefore could date from the same period.

of the 1720s. On the other hand, the softness of the shading and the richness of the chromatic passages also relate it to pastels Rosalba produced in 1720–21 while in Paris. The woman's hair, for example, is rendered in the same way as that of Louis XV as a young boy (fig. 3). Although the identity of the young woman is not known, it is probable that she was English. She resembles closely one of the daughters of Lord Manchester as portrayed by Pellegrini in 1713 in a painting now at Kimbolton Castle (fig. 12).

In the Chicago pastel, the relationship between the young woman and the bird can be explained as participating in the Rococo taste for depicting small and exotic animals, but greater emphasis should be placed on the pastel's allegorical content. The visual arts, like literature, have often represented moral, religious, and scientific concepts by means of symbolic personification. Increasingly, in the eighteenth century, efforts were made to trace the origin of allegorical representations back to classical art. However, the painters of the period, rather than turning directly to classical tradition as the source of their allegories, relied on the vast literary production on allegorical themes, emblems, and iconologies generated during the Renaissance and widely distributed during the Baroque period. The principal text to which they turned was Cesare Ripa's *Iconologia* (first published in 1593).[13]

Rosalba Carriera painted not only portraits in pastel but also heads, or busts, that, for the most part, cannot be easily associated with an identifiable person but that are often invested with allegorical significance. In this area of her activity, she seems to have relied at times on Ripa to establish her subject's attributes precisely. For example, in her *Allegory of Air* (fig. 11), we encounter a healthy and beautiful woman and a dove, which, according to Ripa, is the symbol of the purity of air.[14] In another example, *Vigilance* (fig. 13), the female figure is accompanied, as Ripa dictated for this subject, by a rooster.[15] Rosalba treated the subject of a girl with a dove in a pastel and in two miniatures (see fig. 14).[16] The theme is also found in two canvases by the Bolognese painter Giuseppe Maria Crespi (see fig. 15).[17] In these instances, Rosalba and Crespi seem to have been demonstrating Ripa's connection of a dove to the purity of air and, by reference, to that of the sitter.

Ripa is not very helpful in determining the meaning of the parrot and its gesture in the Chicago pastel; he discussed this bird as a symbol of docility because he considered its ability to repeat human words to be submissive. However, in Rosalba's work, the parrot's gesture, which reveals the woman's breast, is anything but passive and confers on the piece a strongly immodest note. Thus, the parrot in this painting may have a significance closer

FIGURE 11. Rosalba Carriera. *Allegory of Air*, 1746. Pastel on paper; 48.5 x 40 cm. Dresden, Gemäldegalerie. In "fancy" pieces, such as this, often allegorical in nature, Rosalba depicted beautiful women in coquettish poses, their breasts bare or partially covered by diaphanous drapery. The images' symbolic meaning is indicated by an attribute, in this case a dove, which symbolizes the purity of air.

FIGURE 12. Antonio Pellegrini (Italian, 1676–1741). *The Children of Lord Manchester*, 1713. Huntingdonshire, England, Kimbolton Castle. Photo: Courtauld Institute of Art.

to that which Ripa attributed to the sparrow, a symbol of lust. The scene would therefore symbolize something like the loss of virginity, a subject found in certain paintings by the Dutch masters van Mieris and Schalcken and by the French artists Boucher and Le Peintre.[18] In these examples, however, a bird is seen escaping from its cage. Thus, Ripa was not always followed to the letter but often provided basic elements that were then freely interpreted by the artist. If the meaning of *Young Lady with a Parrot* is the loss of virginity, is it possible to consider it a portrait and to search for the identity of the subject, as I have attempted previously?[19] Would a woman of the eighteenth century have allowed a portrait to allude to such an important and intimate event in her life? This is difficult to accept, even if the picture had been painted on the occasion of a wedding, since it is highly doubtful that such an event would have been immortalized in such a bizarre and playful manner. More likely, the interaction

here is a kind of play. In formulating this image, the painter may have been thinking of classical literature, in particular, the poetry of Catullus. The beautiful young woman could be the celebrated Lesbia who, in a famous poem by Catullus, holds a sparrow to her breast and offers him her finger:

Sparrow, my girl's pet,
With whom she is accustomed to play,
Whom she holds to her breast,
To whom, seeking, she extends her finger tip
and provokes to sharp bites.[20]

The love of play, together with a taste for the exotic and for sensual pleasure, was deeply engrained in eighteenth-century culture and created a liking for classical literary works expressing similar sympathies.

This hypothesis, however intriguing, may seem far-fetched, since it presumes that the work of Catullus was

FIGURE 13. Rosalba Carriera. *Vigilance*, c. 1735. Pastel on board; 71 x 55 cm. Stuttgart, Staatsgalerie. The *Iconologia*, a Renaissance lexicon of symbols compiled by Cesare Ripa, was for centuries an influential resource for artists. Here, Rosalba, following Ripa, included a rooster to indicate vigilance.

FIGURE 14. Rosalba Carriera. *Girl with a Dove*. Tempera on ivory; 7 x 5.2 cm. Munich, Bayerisches Nationalmuseum.

sufficiently widespread to furnish specific subjects for painters. And, assuming it was, we must ask how conscious was Rosalba's transposition of a literary theme into painting and whether she would have been capable of such deliberate reiteration. Some notes found among the rough drafts of her correspondence establish that Rosalba, along with her sister Giovanna, had received an education that ranged from Latin to French, a rare occurrence for women of this period. Moreover, she and her sisters had relatives and friends in Padua and frequented this important humanist center. In the first half of the eighteenth century, Padua was home to Antonio Volpi, founder of a printing house that published the work of the greatest Italian and Latin poets, including Lucretius, Catullus, Tibullus, Propertius, Dante, and Petrarch.

It is not clear how extensive Rosalba's learning was—whether it was rudimentary or, as her very cultivated correspondents, such as the English literary figure Joseph Spence, assumed, highly refined and personal. Nonetheless, Rosalba was, in fact, the focus of much poetic activity: friends and admirers of her art addressed poems to her, at times to thank her for the gift of a work, at others to express their love of her paintings. To celebrate her talent for conversation, singing, music, and, above all, painting, Pierre Jean Mariette dedicated a sonnet to her in Italian that opens with allusions to the etymology of the name Rosalba: "Tell me Gentle Rose / serene Dawn, / Did Earth or Sky give you such beautiful names?" and concludes with hyperbolic praise of her painting, expressed in Baroque tercets: "But if I admire the Industry of your Brush, / I swear that a second Apelles lives in You, or that your Images came from heaven. / In such vivid lines I lose myself; go Rose to adorn with miniatures the sun's cycle, / Now that Dawn, your colors have given Light to the world."[21] More unusual are the verses of an unknown admirer thanking the painter for having given him one of her most original compositions (now lost), in which a dead butterfly was shown in the halo of a lighted candle: "So that in my memory will remain impressed / Of an extinct butterfly the bitter fate / From your hand, rare and ingenious birth / I hold manifest, Rosalba, the fatal light."[22]

In both Venetian and international circles, amateur poets were not the only ones to draft verses inspired by Rosalba's paintings; even poets such as the Venetian Gaspare Gozzi confided to the artist in poetry their amorous suffering: "May envy spread its poison and bite and sting / As it wishes my happy love, / For whatever she may do, or say out of disdain / Will not distance me from my first thought." Gozzi even went so far as to communicate to Rosalba reflections of a moral kind: "Oh thou of noble nature above all other creatures / Man born to do good and avoid evil; / Hear me; and if you do not hear me,

FIGURE 15. Giuseppe Maria Crespi (Italian, 1665–1747). *Girl with a Black Dove.* Oil on canvas; 64.6 x 48.3 cm. Columbia, South Carolina, The Columbia Museum of Art.

your beautiful aspect / will turn into the horrible and evil aspect of a beast."[23]

Even these few examples are more than sufficient to help us conclude that, in an environment in which poetry and painting interacted so strongly, portraits by Rosalba Carriera could resonate with literary and even classical references. The relationship here between literature and art seems to have taken the form of a refined game of mirrors, through which style was determined not only as sublimation of the pictorial technique, but also as refined allusion to fact, idea, symbol, and feeling, often poetic in origin.

Notes

LIPPINCOTT, "A Masterpiece of Renaissance Drawing: A *Sacrificial Scene* by Gian Francesco de' Maineri," pp. 6–21.

1. The earlier attributions of the Chicago drawing to Ercole de' Roberti include: *Descriptive Catalogue of the Drawings. . .in the Possession of the Hon. A. E. Gathorne-Hardy* (London, 1902), no. 39; J. Schönbrunner and J. Meder, *Handzeichnungen alter Meister aus der Albertina und anderen Sammlungen*, 12 vols. (Vienna, 1896–1908), vol. 9, no. 1046; *The Vasari Society for the Reproduction of Drawings by Old Masters*, vol. 5 (Oxford, 1908–09), no. 15; E. G. Gardner, *The Painters of Ferrara* (London, 1911), p. 224; G. Gronau, "Ercole (di Giulio Cesare) Grandi," in U. Thieme and F. Willis, *Allgemeines Lexikon der Bildenden Künstler*, vol. 14 (Leipzig, 1921), p. 507; London, Royal Academy, *Exhibition of Italian Art, 1200–1900* (1930), exh. cat., p. 297, no. 610; Lord Balniel and Kenneth Clark, *A Commemorative Catalogue of the Exhibition of Italian Art Held in the Galleries of the Royal Academy, Burlington House, London, January-March, 1930* (London, 1931), p. 239, no. 752; A. E. Popham, *Italian Drawings Exhibited at the Royal Academy, Burlington House, London, 1930* (London, 1931), p. 42, no. 150, pl. 129; N. Barbantini, *Catalogo della esposizione della pittura ferrarese del Rinascimento* (Ferrara, 1933), p. 198, no. 239; Roberto Longhi, *Officina ferrarese* (Florence, 1934), p. 170 n. 89; F. Saxl, "Pagan Sacrifice in the Italian Renaissance," *The Journal of the Warburg and Courtauld Institutes* 2 (1938–39), p. 352 and fig. 61b; S. Ortolani, *Tura, Cossa, Roberto* (Milan, 1941), p. 191; M. Salmi, *Ercole de' Roberti* (Milan, 1960), p. 45, pl. 51; and Eberhard Ruhmer, "Ercole de' Roberti," *Encyclopedia of Universal Art*, vol. 11 (Venice and Rome, 1963), col. 621; and idem, "Ercole de' Roberti," *Encyclopedia of World Art*, vol. 12 (London, 1966), col. 229.

2. For reasons stemming back to the sixteenth century and a mistake in Giorgio Vasari's *Lives of the Painters*, scholars, until recently, thought that the painter we now call Ercole de' Roberti was two different individuals: an earlier artist who painted very much like Cosimo Tura, called "Ercole di Antonio de' Roberti" ("Ercole, son of Antonio, from the Roberti family"); and another, who was believed to be a Bolognese pupil of Lorenzo Costa named "Ercole di Giulio Cesare Grandi" ("Ercole Grandi, the son of Giulio Cesare Grandi"). This muddle was worsened by the fact that many documents referred simply to "Ercole da Ferrara" ("Ercole from Ferrara"), particularly since the experts could not agree whether "Ercole di Giulio Cesare Grandi" was from Ferrara or Bologna.

The numerous scholarly articles written with the sole aim of distinguishing the one Ercole from the other ignored the fact that, in 1864, the great Ferrarese archivist Luigi Napoleone Cittadella had published a document referring to a single Ferrarese painter as "Magistri Erculis de Rubertis alias de Grandis, pictor et civis Ferrariae" ("Master Ercole de' Roberti, also known as being from the Grandi family, painter and Ferrarese citizen"). See L. N. Cittadella, *Notizie relative a Ferrara per la maggior parte inedite* (Ferrara, 1864), p. 589. The idea of two Ercoles was so ingrained in the art-historical imagination that Cittadella himself believed the notation actually confirmed that there were two separate Ercoles: Ercole de' Roberti-Grandi, the painter; and Ercole de' Grandi, the painter and architect. This document, in fact, tells us, or so most now believe, that there was only one Ercole; his double name reflected the fact that his father was from the Roberti family and his mother was a Grandi. It was not at all unusual for artists to use their mothers' names. For example, in the mid-seventeenth century, Artemisia Gentileschi used her mother's family name, Lomi, when painting in Florence, rather than that of her father, the painter Orazio Gentileschi, probably to maximize the possible benefit of her mother's Tuscan origins.

3. Longhi (note 1), pp. 121ff. *Officina ferrarese* was reprinted as part of Longhi's *Opera completa*, vol. 5 (Florence, 1956); see pp. 72–73. This expanded work was itself reprinted as the *Officina ferrarese* (Florence, 1975); see pp. 97–99. See also Longhi's notes on the *Pala Strozzi* in "Ampliamenti nell'Officina ferrarese," *Critica d'arte*, suppl. 4 (1940), esp. pp. 25–27; reprinted in the 1956 *Officina ferrarese*, pp. 152–54, and in the 1975 *Officina ferrarese*, pp. 188–92.

4. See Philip Pouncey, "Ercole Grandi's Masterpiece," *The Burlington Magazine* 70 (1937), pp. 161–68.

5. The attribution by Pouncey first appeared in London, P & D. Colnaghi, *Loan Exhibition of Drawings by Old Masters from the Collection of Mr Geoffrey Gathorne-Hardy* (1971), no. 8, pl. 6.

6. The relevant documents concerning Maineri's career appear in Cittadella (note 2), p. 590; idem, *Documenti ed illustrazioni riguardanti la storia artistica ferrarese* (Ferrara, 1868), pp. 127–28; G. Campori, "I pittori degli Estensi nel secolo XV," in *Atti e memorie della RR deputazione di storia patria per le provincie modenesi e parmensi*, ser. 3, 3 (1885), pp. 525–604 (also published as *Artisti degli Estensi: I pittori* [Modena, 1875], esp. pp. 60–61, 78–79; and reprinted with the same title in Sala Bolognese, 1980, same pagination); A. Venturi, "Gian Francesco de' Maineri pittore," *Archivio storico dell'arte* 1 (1888), pp. 88–90; and in A. Luzio, *La Galleria dei Gonzaga venduta all' Inghilterra nel 1627–28* (Milan, 1913), pp. 196–98.

The best summary of Maineri's work and career can be found in Silla Zamboni, *Pittori di Ercole I d'Este: Giovan Francesco Maineri—Lazzaro Grimaldi—Domenico Panetti—Michele Coltellini* (Milan, 1975), pp. 10–23, 39–61. The artist's first forename, Giovanni, is generally elided with the second as "Giovan Francesco" or "Gian Francesco." I have chosen to use the latter, since this form most closely approximates the sound of his name as it appears in fifteenth-century documents ("Joanne Francisco de Maineriis de Parma, filio quondam Magistri Petri pictoris, et civis Ferrariae" ["Gian Francesco of the Maineri family from Parma, son of the deceased painter Master Pietro, and a citizen of Ferrara"], cited in Zamboni, p. 39).

7. The letter describing the Strozzi's reaction records that they "subito inclinarano la testa facendo reverenza a Sua Excellenza" ("they immediately bowed their heads out of respect for your Excellency"). See Luzio (note 6), p. 197.

8. Pouncey (note 4), pp. 162–68.

9. The last of these three may date to 1502, coinciding with a documented payment for a head of this saint that the artist had received in February of that year from Ercole I d'Este (Ercole I had commissioned the piece as a gift for the Abbess Beatified Sister Lucia da Narni, a miracle-working mystic whom the duke apparently had kidnapped in the hopes that she might be canonized to sainthood, thereby providing Ferrara with its first, and much-needed, "local" saint). Since Maineri habitually repeated his compositions, however, it is virtually impossible to say whether the Brera *Head of Saint John the Baptist* is indeed the painting commissioned for the duke. For more about Ercole I d'Este and the abbess, see L. A. Gandini, *Sulla venuta in Ferrara della B. Suor Lucia da Narni* (Modena, 1901).

10. Similar paintings of the Holy Family can be seen in the Museo di San Giuseppe, Bologna; the Gemäldegalerie, Berlin-Dahlem; the Wernher Collection, Luton Hoo, Bedfordshire; the Museo del Prado, Madrid; and in paintings that were formerly in the Molinari Collection, Cremona; the Civic Museum, Gotha; and the Kunsthaus Lempertz, Cologne.

Versions of Christ Carrying the Cross are in the Taddei Collection, Ferrara; the Galleria degli Uffizi, Florence; the Museo di Palazzo d'Arco, Mantua; the Galleria e Museo Estense, Modena; the Galleria Doria Pamphilj, Rome; the Statens Museum for Kunst, Copenhagen; and formerly in the Carter Collection, Florence. For additional information about these pictures' provenance and the scholarly literature on them, see Zamboni (note 6).

11. For more information about the commission by Clara Clavell of an altarpiece for her family chapel in the Ferrarese church of Santo Spirito, see Campori (note 6), p. 603; and Venturi (note 6), pp. 88–89. I am grateful to Dr. Catherine Turrill of Dartmouth College for informing me that the documents list the patron's last name as "Clavell," rather than "Clavee," as is often repeated in the secondary literature.

12. This suggestion was first made by Longhi (note 3) (1956 ed.), pp. 181–82.

13. Ibid., p. 182: "supplita...dal suo allievo più decadente e lambiccato." Further information about the Art Institute's *Madonna and Child* will be included in the forthcoming catalogue by Christopher Lloyd of the Art Institute's fifteenth- and sixteenth-century Italian paintings.

14. Compare, for example, the broad jawlines and small, pointed chins of Maineri's figures with those found in Cossa's heads on the eastern wall of the Salone dei Mesi in the Palazzo Schifanoia in Ferrara.

15. See Pouncey (note 4); Zamboni (note 6), pp. 11–12, 56, and no. 33; V. I. Stoichita, "Deux Oeuvres ferraraises au Musée d'Art de la République Socialiste de Roumanie," *Revue romaine d'histoire de l'art* 15 (1978), pp. 19–52; esp. p. 41 and fig. 23; and Maria Grazia Vaccaro's catalogue entry in A. Boschetto, ed., *Maestri emiliani del Quattro e Cinquecento*, vol. 11 of *Biblioteca di Disegni* (Florence, 1980), no. 1.

16. For an overview of the topic, see Michael Hirst, "The Making of Presents," in *Michelangelo and His Drawings* (New Haven, Conn., and London, 1988), pp. 105–18.

17. For reproductions and a discussion, from a slightly different point of view, see R. Lightbown, *Mantegna* (Oxford, 1986), esp. pp. 210–18 and 227–33.

18. The *Danaë* on loan to the Art Institute (loan no. 9.1973), for example, is most likely a workshop product, with the hand of Titian evident only in some finishing touches in the landscape and in the flesh of Danaë.

19. Also relevant here is Vittorio Carpaccio's drawing *Saint Augustine in His Study* in the British Museum, London (1934–12–8–1). The best overview of fifteenth-century drawing techniques appears in Francis Ames-Lewis, *Drawing in Early Renaissance Italy* (New Haven, Conn., and London, 1981); and Nottingham, University Art Gallery, and London, Victoria and Albert Museum, *Drawing in the Italian Renaissance Workshop*, exh. cat. by Francis Ames-Lewis and Joanne Wright (1983).

20. The antiquarian drawings in the Modena manuscript (Modena, Biblioteca Estense, cod. lat. 992 [αL.5.15]) have long been attributed to Felice Feliciano. See, for example, Silvia Danesi Squarzina, "Eclisse del gusto cortese e nascita della cultura antiquaria: Ciriaco, Feliciano, Marcanova, Alberti," in *Da Pisanello alla nascita dei Musei Capitolini. L'antico a Roma alla vigilia del Rinascimento*, exh. cat. (Milan and Rome, 1988), pp. 27–37. Recently, however, one Italian scholar has suggested that the fanciful classical scenes included in the manuscript are by another hand, possibly that of the Paduan Marco Zoppo or one of his immediate circle. See M. T. Fiorio, "Marco Zoppo et le livre

padouan," *Revue de l'art* 53 (1981), pp. 65–77. I thank Michael Koortbojian for discussing these drawings with me.

21. See E. H. Gombrich, *Art and Illusion* (London, 1960), chap. 2.

22. Saxl (note 1), p. 352, n. 4.

23. Other Emilian artists whose paintings include pagan/Old Testament insets include Tura, Aspertini, Grimaldi, Mazzolino, and Munari.

24. Pouncey's suggestion (note 4) has been widely accepted. See, for example, R. Varese, *Lorenzo Costa* (Milan, 1967), pp. 37–38, 71; Zamboni (note 6), pp. 16–17, 47–49; London, National Gallery, *The National Gallery Illustrated Catalogue* (London, 1973), p. 131, no. 1119; and C. Gould, *National Gallery Catalogues, The Sixteenth-Century Italian Schools* (London, 1975), pp. 77–80.

GILES, "*Christ before Pilate*: A Major Composition Study by Pontormo," pp. 22–40.

I would like to thank the following individuals for their generous assistance with various aspects of this article: Jonathan Bober, Eve Borsook, Anselmo Carini, Rachel Dressler, Douglas Druick, John and Marjorie Giles, George Goldner, Sarah Kianovsky, Suzanne McCullagh, Robert Miller, Dirk Shears, Miriam Stewart, Harriet Stratis, John Tedeschi, Martha Tedeschi, Claire Van Cleave, and Martha Wolff.

1. This drawing was acquired from the British Rail Pension Fund.

2. This number is based on Janet Cox-Rearick's *The Drawings of Pontormo: A Catalogue Raisonné with Notes on the Paintings*, 2 vols. (New York, 1981). Allowing for additions to and deletions from the first edition (*The Drawings of Pontormo* [Cambridge, 1964]), the revised number of drawings considered autograph by Cox-Rearick is 416.

3. In addition to the Art Institute study, these are: two drawings (on one sheet) in The Pierpont Morgan Library, New York (Cox-Rearick [note 2], nos. 188–189); three drawings (on two sheets) in the Fogg Art Museum, Cambridge, Massachusetts (Cox-Rearick [note 2], nos. 139, 151, 340); and eight drawings (on five sheets) in the J. Paul Getty Museum of Art, Malibu, California. For six of the Getty drawings, see Cox-Rearick (note 2), nos. 38, 48a, 60, 67a; and Malibu, California, The J. Paul Getty Museum of Art, *European Drawings: Catalogue of the Collections*, exh. cat. by George R. Goldner (1988), nos. 34–35.

4. When Julien Stock saw the drawing, it was still laid down on a cream laid-paper mount with a hand-colored decorative border, on the back of which was inscribed in graphite and in three different hands: *circa 1670/not Carracci* (upper left); *Carracci* (middle center); *Agos. Carracci* (lower center). Ultraviolet examination in the Paper Conservation Laboratory at The Art Institute of Chicago revealed an inscription on the verso of the primary support that seemed to read *Pontormo*. When David Chandler, Paper Conservator, debacked the drawing in the course of treating it, such an inscription was confirmed, written in pen and brown ink and in a seventeenth-century, or perhaps later, hand.

5. It should be acknowledged that Janet Cox-Rearick has verbally confirmed the authenticity of the drawing on the basis of a photograph and has dated it to the early 1520s.

6. The information on Pontormo's formative years and on his life as a whole derives primarily from Giorgio Vasari's biography, contained in his *Le vite de' più eccellenti pittori, scultori ed architetti*, 2 vols. (Florence, 1568). The standard edition of this work is by Gaetano Milanesi, ed., 9 vols. (Florence, 1878–85), hereinafter called Vasari-Milanesi. Most of the English translations from Vasari's *Vite* that appear in this article are from *Lives of the Most Eminent Painters, Sculptors, and Architects*, trans. Gaston du C. De Vere, 3 vols. (New York, 1979).

The first monograph on Pontormo was Frederick Mortimer Clapp's *Jacopo Carucci da Pontormo: His Life and Work* (New Haven, Conn., 1916). In 1956, a major exhibition in Florence commemorating the 400th anniversary of the artist's death (Luciano Berti, et al., *Mostra del Pontormo e del primo Manierismo Fiorentino*, exh. cat. [Florence: Palazzo Strozzi, 1956]) generated a group of Pontormo studies, including Cox-Rearick's catalogue raisonné of the drawings (note 2), and two monographs: Luciano Berti, *Pontormo* (Florence, 1964), and Kurt W. Forster, *Pontormo: Monographie mit Kritischem Katalog* (Munich, 1966). Also worthy of mention is Berti's fully illustrated *L'opera completa del Pontormo* (Milan, 1973).

The earliest discussion of Pontormo's draftsmanship is found in Bernard Berenson's pioneering *Drawings of the Florentine Painters* (London, 1903), 2nd rev. ed., vol. 1 (Chicago, 1938), pp. 300–321. Berenson's elimination of many of the drawings attributed to Pontormo was continued by F. M. Clapp in his *Dessins de Pontormo* (Paris, 1914) and subsequently by Cox-Rearick in her 1964 catalogue raisonné (note 2). Also worth noting is L. Berti, *Pontormo: I Disegni* (Florence, 1965).

See also Sydney J. Freedberg, *Painting of the High Renaissance in Rome and Florence*, vol. 1 (Cambridge, Mass., 1961), and idem, *Painting in Italy 1500–1600*, rev. ed. (Harmondsworth, 1971), for concise discussions of Pontormo as a painter and draftsman.

7. See Freedberg, *Painting in Italy* (note 6), pp. 14–31, for a concise discussion of Leonardo in the context of Florentine painting.

8. Although the altarpiece has been called the *Deposition* by all Pontormo scholars from Clapp (note 6) onwards, John Shearman has convincingly argued that this title is inaccurate in *Pontormo's Altarpiece in S. Felicità (The 51st Charlton Lecture, 1968)* (Newcastle upon Tyne, 1971).

9. De Vere (note 6), vol. 3, p. 1542; Vasari-Milanesi (note 6), vol. 6, p. 289: "e fu oltre ogni credenza solitario."

10. There is a vast literature on Mannerism. The best introduction to this complex subject is John Shearman's *Mannerism* (Harmondsworth, 1967). Of relevance in understanding Pontormo's place in this context is the second chapter, "The Arrival of Mannerism in the Visual Arts," pp. 49–79.

11. Freedberg, *Painting in Italy* (note 6), p. 184, noted that Pontormo had previously inserted himself as a major actor in his lunette fresco *The Road to Calvary* of 1523/24 (ibid., fig. 73), where he is shown helping the fallen Christ lift his cross.

12. Vasari-Milanesi (note 6), vol. 1, p. 168.

13. For a concise discussion of this procedure, see Charles de Tolnay, *History and Technique of Old Master Drawings: A Handbook* (New York, 1943).

14. De Vere (note 6), vol. 3, p. 1528; Vasari-Milanesi (note 6), vol. 6, p. 269: "Besides this, he painted for the room of the Prior of that place a picture of the Nativity of Christ, representing Joseph as giving light to Jesus Christ in the darkness of the night with a lantern."

Cox-Rearick (note 2), no. 194, dated the drawing c. 1522 and related it to an oblong *Adoration of the Magi* panel painting (Florence, Palazzo Pitti), which has generally been dated slightly earlier (see Berti, *L'opera completa* [note 6], no. 66, pls. 24–27). Although the lantern held by Joseph described by Vasari in his discussion of the Certosa painting is absent in the Uffizi drawing, I agree with Berti, *Pontormo: I Disegni* (note 6), no. 33, that it represents a first idea for the lost Nativity.

15. Cox-Rearick (note 2), no. 224. Prior to Cox-Rearick, Clapp, *Dessins de Pontormo* (note 6), no. 225, thought that the drawing might be a study for a lost painting of Saint George, while Berenson (note 6), no. 2160, connected the composition with the *Legend of the 10,000 Martyrs* of 1529/30 in the Palazzo Pitti, Florence (see Berti, *L'opera completa* [note 6], no. 111, pl. 60).

16. See E. H. Gombrich, "Leonardo's Method for Working out Compositions," in *Norm and Form: Studies in the Art of the Renaissance* (London, 1966), pp. 58–63.

17. For illustrations of the verso (British Museum Inv. 1875–6–12–7 verso), see Gombrich (note 16), fig. 95, and A. E. Popham and Philip Pouncey, *Italian Drawings in the Department of Prints and Drawings in the British Museum: The Fourteenth and Fifteenth Centuries*, vol. 2 (London, 1950), pl. 107.

18. The dates for the execution of the frescoes have been established on the basis of a document in the account books of the Certosa that records payments to Pontormo for his frescoes in the cloister from February 4, 1523, to April 10, 1524. See Clapp, *Jacopo Carucci* (note 6), app. 2, doc. 16, p. 278.

In addition to two lost works painted while at the Certosa—the *Nativity* and a fresco portrait of a 120-year-old lay brother (Vasari-Milanesi [note 6], vol. 6, p. 269)—Pontormo executed a *Supper at Emmaus* panel painting for the refectory, inscribed 1525 and now in the Uffizi (see Berti, *L'opera completa* [note 6], no. 85, pls. 39–41).

19. De Vere (note 6), vol. 3, p. 1525; Vasari-Milanesi (note 6), vol. 6, p. 266: "Then in the year 1522, there being a slight outbreak of plague in Florence... an occasion presented itself to Jacopo of flying the city and removing himself to some distance, for a certain Prior of the Certosa...had to have some pictures painted in fresco at the corners of a very large and beautiful cloister that surrounds a lawn, and Jacopo was brought to his notice; whereupon the Prior had him sought out, and he, having accepted the work willingly at such a time, went off to [the] Certosa, taking with him only Bronzino."

20. For the most comprehensive and well-illustrated history of the Certosa and its art, see Caterina Chiarelli and Giovanni Leoncini, *La Certosa del Galluzzo a Firenze* (Milan, 1982).

21. De Vere (note 6), vol. 3, pp. 1525, 1527; Vasari-Milanesi (note 6), vol. 6, pp. 266, 269. As Clapp, *Jacopo Carucci* (note 6), p. 40, first noted, confirmation of this assertion is found in one of the final entries in Pontormo's diary (transcribed ibid., app. 3, p. 307). On October 11, 1556, two months before his death, he wrote that he had gone to the Certosa on Sunday ("domenica andai a certosa").

22. De Vere (note 6), vol. 3, p. 1526; Vasari-Milanesi (note 6), vol. 6, p. 267: "che la vaghezza della sua prima maniera, la quale gli era stata data dalla natura, tutta piena di dolcezza e di grazia, venne alterata da quel nuovo studio e fatica e cotanto offesa dall'accidente di quella tedesca, che non si conosce

in tutte quest'opere, come che tutte sien belle, se non poco di quel buono e grazia che egli aveva insino allora dato a tutte le sue figure."

23. In his discussion of the Certosa Passion cycle (Vasari-Milanesi [note 6], vol. 6, pp. 266–69), Vasari departed from both the narrative sequence and the physical placement of the frescoes in the cloister (*Agony in the Garden, Christ before Pilate, Road to Calvary, Pietà,* and *Resurrection*) in commenting on the *Resurrection* after *Christ before Pilate* and before the *Road to Calvary.* As noted by Cox-Rearick (note 2), p. 214 nn. 16, 19, Vasari may have known the order in which the frescoes were executed, as he himself was there in 1524, according to a passage in his life of Bronzino, who worked at the Certosa as Pontormo's assistant. Vasari wrote that he met his friend Bronzino at the Certosa in 1524, when he visited the cloister in order to draw from the frescoes (Vasari-Milanesi [note 6], vol. 7, p. 605).

For illustrations of all the Certosa frescoes, see Berti, *L'opera completa* (note 6), nos. 78–82, pls. 32–36, and Chiarelli and Leoncini (note 20), figs. 20–26. For discussions of the frescoes, see Cox-Rearick (note 2), pp. 213–17; Clapp, *Jacopo Carucci* (note 6), pp. 37–41; Forster (note 6), pp. 48–57; and Paula Beckers, *Die Passionsfresken Pontormos für die Certosa del Galluzzo,* 2 vols. (Salzburg, 1985).

24. De Vere (note 6), vol. 3, p. 1526; Vasari-Milanesi (note 6), vol. 6, pp. 267–68.

25. As noted by Cox-Rearick (note 2), p. 215, several elements, including the crowding of the soldiers and the slender figure of Christ, derive from the woodcut of *Christ before Herod* in the *Small Passion* (see fig. 13). For *Christ before Herod* (Bartsch 32) and subsequent images from the *Small Passion,* see Adam von Bartsch, *Le Peintre-graveur,* 21 vols. and suppl. (Vienna, 1803–21). Clapp, *Jacopo Carucci* (note 6), p. 109, was the first to suggest that the half-length soldiers derived from Dürer's woodcut *The Bathing House* of c.1496 (Bartsch 128; illustrated in Walter Strauss, ed., *Albrecht Dürer: Woodcuts and Woodblocks* [New York, 1980], no. 31).

26. Irving Lavin, "An Observation on 'Medievalism' in Early Sixteenth Century Style," *Gazette des beaux-arts,* ser. 6, 50 (1957), pp. 113–18.

27. Beckers (note 23).

28. As first noted by Giovanni Leoncini, *La Certosa di Firenze nei suoi rapporti con l'Architettura Certosina* (Salzburg, 1979), p. 172 n. 155, there is a record of payment dated July 10, 1483, for fifteen books purchased from the Certosa di Pavia, including "2 volumi de Vita Christi." For a transcription of the payment, see Caterina Chiarelli, *Le attività artistiche e il patrimonio librario della Certosa di Firenze,* vol. 2 (Salzburg, 1984), p. 312.

29. These are listed in the *Gesamtkatalog der Wiegendrucke,* vol. 4 (Leipzig, 1930), nos. 4769–97.

30. "& intrando iesu in nel palacio se inclinavano insino a terra gli dodeci standardi liquali gurdavano el pretorio & non per la sua voluntate ma per paura forono costreti ingenochiarse & adorare: la qualcosa vede[n]do pilato tutto impaurito usci di fora." See the *Meditatione sopra la passione del nostro signore iesu christo* (Venice, Matteo Capcasa, March 10, 1492), sig. ci. This edition is listed as no. 4774 in the *Gesamtkatalog* (note 29). I consulted a copy of this edition in The Newberry Library, Chicago (Inc. 4992.5).

For the relevant section in the Gospel of Nicodemus from which the passage in the *Meditatione* is derived, see Montague Rhodes James, *The Apocryphal New Testament* (Oxford, 1926), pp. 97–98.

31. It should be noted that thus far I have not located any other illustrations of the miraculous scene with the standards. Assuming that Pontormo was familiar with the *Meditatione,* it is worth considering whether the particular edition he used contained such an image. Of the two editions with which I am familiar (that of Venice, 1492, and one printed in Florence, 1495), neither illustrates the miraculous occurrence. As most of the editions do include woodcut illustrations, further research is needed. I am grateful to Karen Davidson for consulting the Florence, 1495, edition, a copy of which is housed in the Pierpont Morgan Library, New York.

It is possible that a visual precedent for this scene might be found in contemporary passion plays, an area that requires further research on my part. Pontormo's familiarity with and possible involvement in a sacred play concerning the Annunciation has been discussed by Frederick A. Cooper in "Jacopo Pontormo and Influences from the Renaissance Theater," *Art Bulletin* 11 (1973), pp. 380–92.

32. For discussions of the transformation of Pontormo's compositional ideas for *Vertumnus and Pomona,* see Cox-Rearick (note 2), pp. 40–44; Freedberg, *Painting of the High Renaissance* (note 6), pp. 562–63.

33. De Vere (note 6), vol. 3, p. 1524; Vasari-Milanesi (note 6), vol. 6, pp. 264–65: "perciocchè guastando e rifacendo oggi quello che aveva fatto ieri, si travagliava di maniera il cervello, che era una compassione; ma tuttavia andava sempre facendo nuovi trovati, con onor suo e bellezza dell'opera."

34. See Cox-Rearick (note 2), nos. 131–60. There is also an unpublished preparatory study for *Vertumnus and Pomona* in the J. Paul Getty Museum.

35. See Cox-Rearick (note 2), nos. 196–214.

36. There are two studies of a figure seen from the back on a study sheet in the Uffizi (Cox-Rearick [note 2], no. 227) that remotely resemble the taller figure of Christ in the Art Institute study. Cox-Rearick considered the sheet to be related to the *Israelites Drinking the Water in the Wilderness.* It should be noted that most of the 378 drawings that Cox-Rearick designated as "attributed" are not reproduced. It is possible that an examination of this group may unearth figure studies related to the Art Institute drawing.

37. De Vere (note 6), vol. 3, p. 1527; Vasari-Milanesi (note 6), vol. 6, p. 269: "After these he was to have gone on with the Crucifixion and the Deposition from the Cross in the other corners."

38. Cox-Rearick (note 2), p. 222, has noted the dependence of the *Nailing to the Cross* on Dürer's woodcut of the subject (Bartsch 39) in the *Small Passion* (illustrated in Strauss [note 25], no. 123), while Clapp, *Jacopo Carucci* (note 6), p. 43, was the first to note the connection between the *Deposition* drawing and Dürer's woodcut of the *Descent from the Cross* (Bartsch 42), also in the *Small Passion* (illustrated in Strauss [note 25], no. 126).

39. Cox-Rearick (note 2), nos. 207, 212.

40. For Andrea del Sarto's fresco cycle in the Chiostro dello Scalzo, see the detailed discussions and illustrations in Sydney J. Freedberg, *Andrea del Sarto* (Cambridge, Mass., 1963), and John Shearman, *Andrea del Sarto* (Oxford, 1965). See also Eve Borsook's concise discussion in *The Mural Painters of Tuscany from Cimabue to Andrea del Sarto,* 2nd ed. (Oxford, 1980), pp. 127–31.

41. Shearman (note 40), vol. 1, pp. 68–69; vol. 2, pp. 301–302. As Shearman has noted, Freedberg (note 40), vol. 1, pp. 41–42, argued that the resemblance between del Sarto's fresco and Raphael's cartoon is fortuitous, and that the

Saint Paul–like figure seen from the rear is "a recurrence and development" of a motif appearing in del Sarto's early paintings onward.

It should be noted that in this fresco del Sarto has borrowed specific motifs from Dürer's prints. In particular, Shearman noted the knotted shawl over the figure seen from the rear, which derives from the woodcut of the *Pentecost* (Bartsch 51) in the *Small Passion* (illustrated in Strauss [note 25], no. 135).

42. For Dürer's *Ascension*, see Bartsch 50.

43. De Vere (note 6), p. 1525; Vasari-Milanesi (note 6), vol. 6, p. 266: "pensò con quella occasione fare nelle cose dell'arti uno sforzo di studio, e mostrare al mondo avere acquistato maggior perfezione, e variata maniera da quelle cose che aveva fatta prima."

STRATIS, "The Technical Aspects of Pontormo's *Christ before Pilate*," pp. 47–51.

I thank Konstanze Bachmann, David Chandler, Anne Driesse, Douglas Druick, Laura Giles, Matthew Glucksberg, and Sarah Kianovsky for useful discussions and suggestions; Frank Zuccari for sharing his expertise in infrared reflectography; and the Andrew W. Mellon Foundation for providing financial support during the course of this work.

1. Janet Cox-Rearick referred to Pontormo's occasional use of toned papers in the period before 1530, and noted his use of brown, gray, and blue papers specifically, in *The Drawings of Pontormo: A Catalogue Raisonné with Notes on the Paintings*, vol. 1 (New York, 1981), p. 5.

2. C.M. Briquet, *Les Filigranes: Dictionnaire historique des marques du papier des leur apparition vers 1282 jusqu'en 1600* (1907; new ed., Amsterdam, 1968); see esp. vol. 1, pp. 406–07, and vol. 3, no. 7435.

3. Jane Roberts, *A Dictionary of Michelangelo's Watermarks* (Milan, 1988), p. 16 and acorn reproduction. It should be noted that this sheet bears studies by Michelangelo in addition to other studies by another hand.

4. The ten drawings that have an acorn sprig watermark (Briquet [note 2], no. 7435) have the following Cox-Rearick (note 1) catalogue numbers: 143, 145, 155, 159, 160, 161, 162, 174, 178, 225. See p. 4 n. 3, and each individual catalogue entry.

5. In the course of manuscript preparation, five Pontormo drawings were examined firsthand as follows: two drawings (on one sheet), 1954.4, in The Pierpont Morgan Library, New York (Cox-Rearick [note 1], nos. 188 and 189), and three drawings (on two sheets), 1932.144 and 1932.342, in the Fogg Art Museum, Cambridge, Mass. (Cox-Rearick [note 1], nos. 139, 151, and 340).

6. The incised lines on the drawing also could not have been created by transferring media away from the recto to create an incised counterproof. In the process, black chalk passages related to the present composition, and clearly visible over many of the incised lines, would have been removed or diminished. The possibility that the incised lines were transferred from a preliminary drawing with an unblackened verso cannot be completely discounted.

7. For more detailed discussions of Raphael's use of incising in his drawings, see Francis Ames-Lewis, *The Draftsman Raphael* (New Haven, Conn., 1986), and John Shearman, *Raphael's Cartoons in the Collection of Her Majesty the Queen and the Tapestries for the Sistine Chapel* (London, 1972), specifically pp. 101–02.

8. Additional passages of red chalk in the drawing are clearly offset from an unrelated sheet. The red chalk bears no compositional relation to the forms over which it has been offset, nor does it tonally modify them. A sheet of studies for *Vertumnus and Pomona* in the Fogg Art Museum (1932.342 recto) similarly carries faint red chalk offset through much of the drawing.

9. The drawing was examined under infrared light using a vidicon camera equipped with an infrared tube (Grundig Electronic Vidicon Camera, SN 76) that scans the drawing line by line and transmits images of small sections to a black-and-white monitor (Grundig Electronic Monitor BG12, SN 72). Different wavelengths of infrared light, between 900 and 2000 nanometers, are absorbed or reflected to a varying degree by the art object. Light reflected back to the camera by the paper support is transmitted to the monitor in white. Carbon-containing black chalk particles absorb the radiation and the image on the monitor appears black. The high contrast infrared image enhances details of the drawing and provides insight into the artist's methods.

10. The sectional images photographed from the monitor are assembled to create a composite photograph, or reflectogram, of the entire drawing. Differentiated gray tones on the monitor are recorded in the photographs, and when these photographs are joined together, variable tones are visible.

11. Infrared reflectography has been used with increasing frequency in recent years to examine drawings executed in both dry media such as chalk and in liquid media such as ink. For additional studies, see Shelley Fletcher, "A Preliminary Study of the Use of Infrared Reflectography in the Examination of Works on Paper," *The International Council of Museums Preprints* 84, 24 (1984), pp. 24–28; Konrad Renger and Andreas Burmester, "The Munich Rembrandt Forgeries Reconsidered: A New Technical Approach to the Investigation of Drawings," *Master Drawings* 23–24, 4 (1985–86), pp. 526–37; Bruce F. Miller, "Technical Note on the Cleveland Michelangelo Drawing," *The Bulletin of the Cleveland Museum of Art* 77, 5 (May 1989), pp. 175–79; Michael Miller, "A Michelangelo Drawing," ibid., pp. 146–74.

12. All microscopic examination of the drawing was carried out under a Wild M-7 stereo microscope, in the range between 20x to 30x magnification.

13. John Shearman, in his review of Cox-Rearick's catalogue raisonné of the drawings, noted tonal transitions of red chalk in a study for Saint Christopher that he asserted look like wash. See review of *The Drawings of Pontormo: A Catalogue Raisonné with Notes on the Painting*, by Janet Cox-Rearick, *Art Bulletin* 54 (June 1972), p. 211.

14. Although a good deal of chalk has penetrated into the interstices of the paper fibers, only the white chalk passages have become illegible. When first acquired by the Art Institute, the drawing was glued down onto an eighteenth century (?) mount and had sustained some water damage. To reduce water stains, the drawing first had to be removed from this mount. In the course of conservation, the mount was removed intact and retained for archival purposes. Water stains were then reduced, and a loss in the lower left corner of the drawing was filled with a similar paper toned to match. Charcoal reinforcement from an earlier restoration of this area extends into the original drawing directly surrounding the area of loss. In light of the drawing's age and previous restoration, its condition is, overall, quite good.

McCULLAGH, "Serendipity in a Solander Box: A Recently Discovered Pastel and Chalk Drawing by Federico Barocci," pp. 52–65.

This article is dedicated to the memory of Philip Pouncey.

1. Italian artists such as Barocci or Guido Reni found a wide following among British artists of the seventeenth through nineteenth centuries. Sir Peter Lely, Jonathan Richardson the Elder, and Sir Joshua Reynolds, for example, not only collected Italian drawings but also made many figure drawings in colored chalks on tinted paper. For comparison, see Lindsay Stainton and Christopher White, *Drawing in England from Hilliard to Hogarth*, exh. cat. (London, 1987), p. 123, no. 88, and p. 228, no. 182.

2. See, for example, Harald Olsen, *Federico Barocci* (Copenhagen, 1962); Edmund P. Pillsbury and Louise S. Richards, *The Graphic Art of Federico Barocci: Selected Drawings and Prints*, exh. cat. (New Haven, Conn., 1978); Gary R. Walters, *Federico Barocci: Anima Naturaliter* (New York and London, 1978); Andrea Emiliani, *Federico Barocci (Urbino 1535–1612)*, 2 vols. (Bologna, 1985).

3. The distinction between natural colored chalks (primarily red, white, black, and ocher) and man-made pastels is difficult to verify accurately with the naked eye, without scientific analysis of an actual sample of media. Such analysis was not undertaken here because adequate sample was not available for removal from the surface of the drawing. Stereomicroscopy indicates that in his *Christ Child* study, Barocci used red and black natural chalks, ocher pastel (which could well be chalk), and touches of pink that also seem to be pastel. I would like to thank conservator David Chandler for his research and counsel on the media of Barocci's *Christ Child*.

4. I would like to express my gratitude to Edmund Pillsbury, who kindly confirmed my identification of the *Christ Child*, and pointed out the possibility that the drawing might be a life-sized cartoon. I would also like to thank the Soprintendenza dei beni artistici e storici delle Marche, Urbino, for allowing me to compare my mylar tracing of the pastel with the finished altarpiece.

5. Edmund P. Pillsbury, review of *Federico Barocci (Urbino 1535–1612)*, by Andrea Emiliani, *Master Drawings* 25, 3 (Autumn 1987), pp. 286–87.

6. First published by Filippo di Pietro, *Disegni sconosciuti e disegni finora non identificati de Federico Barocci negli Uffizi* (Florence, 1913), p. 4, figs. 4–5.

7. Somewhat confusing the issue is another early study for the *Madonna di San Giovanni* that has recently come to light on the verso of a sheet of studies for the Chiesa Nuova *Visitation* of 1583/86. See David Ekserdjian, review of *Federico Barocci (Urbino 1535–1612)*, by Andrea Emiliani, *Burlington Magazine* 129 (June 1987), pp. 402–403, who first mentions the importance of this drawing sold at Christie's, London (July 1, 1986; lot 114). Executed rapidly in pen and brown ink, brush and brown wash over black chalk, the unusual posture of the half-kneeling form is identical to that of Saint John the Evangelist; in addition, there are minimal but distinct indications of the legs and outreaching arm of the Christ Child. But, as Ekserdjian further pointed out, the kneeling figure in the drawing appears female and seems to be proffering a lamb, denoting instead an *Adoration of the Shepherds* subject. Ekserdjian believed the handling of both sides of the sheet to be "of a piece, and does not suggest that one was done twenty years before the other," thereby implying that Barocci returned to the *Madonna di San Giovanni* motif later on.

Moreover, based on comparison with another early drawing in the British Museum, London, signaled by Pillsbury as a typical *disegno compito*, it would

seem the equivalent stage no longer exists for the *Madonna di San Giovanni*, if there was one (see Pillsbury and Richards [note 2], pp. 40–41, no. 12).

Hitherto unmentioned is a slightly more finished study of the Mother-and-Child group, formerly in the Cammuccini Collection in Orvieto, now known only through a photograph in the Uffizi (reproduced in the documentation in the Gabinetto disegni e stampi as negative no. Sopr. 281409). It appears to focus on the Virgin's robes and would seem to be the sort of elaborate study in chalk that constitutes the preparation for the full-scale cartoon.

8. Pillsbury and Richards (note 2), p. 42, no. 15.

9. G. B. Bellori, *Le Vite dei Pittori, Scultori, e Architetti Moderni* (Rome, 1672), cited in Pillsbury and Richards (note 2), p. 42, no. 15.

10. Pillsbury and Richards (note 2), pp. 42–43, no. 16, and p. 44, no. 1; for studies of the head of Saint John, see Berlin (Dahlem) Kupferstichkabinett, no. 20392 recto, and Stockholm, Nationalmuseum, no. 405/1863 (both unpublished).

11. Pillsbury and Richards (note 2), p. 44, no. 2 (Musée du Louvre 2864, 2865).

12. Remnants of other studies that fall outside Pillsbury's scheme are found under other sketches: the upper portion of the Virgin and Child can be glimpsed under an elaborate compositional *Study for the Crucifixion* of c. 1579 (see Pillsbury and Richards [note 2], p. 45, no. 18; and G. G. Bertelà, *Disegni di Federico Barocci*, exh. cat. [Florence, 1975], pp. 26–27, no. 8, fig. 12 [inv. 11416 F]); and the chalice and saint under a sketch for the *Virgin with Saints Roch and Sebastian* (Chatsworth no. 358; see Pillsbury and Richards [note 2], pp. 44–45, no. 17).

A large drawing of the whole composition in the Albertina, Vienna, has been identified as a study for a woodcut (Emiliani [note 2], p. 64). An unusual landscape sketch in pen and brown ink heightened with white on blue paper, in the Kunsthalle Hamburg, has also been linked with this composition, not entirely convincingly (A. Schmarsow, "Federico Barocci's Zeichnungen," *Abhandlung der Sachsische Akademie der Wissenschaften* 26 [1909], no. 5; 28 [1910], no. 3; 30 [1914], no. 1; see Pillsbury and Richards [note 2], p. 38, no. 10).

13. Baldassare Castiglione, *The Courtier (Il Cortegiano)* (1528), trans. Sir Thomas Hory (1561; reprint: London, 1928).

14. Walters (note 2), p. 36.

15. Olsen (note 2), pp. 19–21, cited Bellori, and offered a good introduction to the artist and his life in English, from which many of these associations and biographical details derive.

16. Although Bassano's work was more or less contemporary with Barocci's—the *Apostle Head* reproduced here (fig. 8) can be linked with the 1570 painting *Descent of the Holy Spirit* in the town of Bassano—the artist "continued a tradition which in Italy had first gained importance in Lombardy and reached another high-point in the 16th century in the work of Barocci"; see Walter Koschatzky, Konrad Oberhuber, and Eckhart Knab, *Italian Drawings in the Albertina* (Greenwich, Conn., 1971), no. 64.

17. Bellori's complete text was first published in an English translation in Pillsbury and Richards (note 2), pp. 13–24; see p. 14 for discussion of the influence of Raphael and Taddeo Zuccaro on Barocci.

18. Ekserdjian (note 7).

19. Walters (note 2), p. 181 n. 37.

20. Graham Smith, *The Casino of Pius IV* (Princeton, N.J., 1977), p. 67. The work was begun in 1561; Barocci was one of the few to be paid, in June 1563.

21. Quoted in Walters (note 2), p. 2.

22. Bellori quoted in Pillsbury and Richards (note 2), p. 15.

23. Rudolf and Margot Wittkower, *Born under Saturn* (New York, 1963), p. 81. According to Pillsbury and Richards (note 2), p. 15, no. 14, the story of the poisoning of the salad came from Vincenzo Borghini in 1584 and Giovanni Baglione in 1642, and, based on Bellori's account, Jorgen Kringelbach diagnosed Barocci's malady as a chronic gastric or peptic ulcer.

24. Bellori quoted in Wittkower (note 23), p. 79.

25. John F. Moffitt, "Painters Born under Saturn: The Physiological Explanations," *Art History* 11, 2 (June 1988), pp. 197–98.

26. See Suzanne Folds McCullagh and Pierre Rosenberg, "The Supreme Triumph of the Old Painter: Chardin's Final Work in Pastel," *The Art Institute of Chicago Museum Studies* 12, 1 (Fall 1985), pp. 43–60.

27. Whereas Leonardo da Vinci may actually have initiated in Italy the pastel technique, Barocci was the first Italian artist to use it extensively and develop it as part of his working procedure. It has been said that "Barocci's use of colored chalks on blue paper is arguably unassailable until the French School" (Ekserdjian [note 7]). On the development in Italy of the pastel medium, see Geneviève Monnier, *Pastels: From the 16th to the 20th Century* (New York, 1984), and, in this issue, Bernardina Sani, "Rosalba Carriera's *Young Lady with a Parrot*," pp. 74–87.

28. Bellori quoted in Pillsbury and Richards (note 2), p. 15.

29. Perhaps the *Madonna di San Giovanni*, Barocci's first oil after his illness, is of a small scale because it was a votive offering, an uncommissioned gift; it may also have been the most ambitious work that the recovering artist would dare take on or could bear to address.

30. Monnier (note 27), p. 13.

31. Bellori quoted in Pillsbury and Richards (note 2), p. 15.

32. David Alan Brown, "Correggio's 'Virgin and Child with the Infant St. John,'" *The Art Institute of Chicago Museum Studies* 7 (1972), pp. 7–34.

33. Olsen (note 2), p. 52, characterized the palette of the painting as "cool blue, green, pink and brown tones, [which with]...the bright light coming from the left...attain a phosphorescent effect similar to that in Ferrarese paintings or Lotto's, whose art was well represented in *Le Marche*." While this, to an extent, is true (see, for example, Lorenzo Lotto's *Nativity* of 1523 in the National Gallery of Art, Washington, D.C.), more important for this issue is the interaction between the color studies and the finished oil.

34. Marilyn Aronberg Lavin, "Colour Study in Barocci's Drawings," *Burlington Magazine* 48 (1956), p. 330.

35. Emiliani (note 2), p. 64.

36. Olsen (note 2), p. 52, called the *Madonna di San Giovanni* "a corrected and more concentrated version of the Holy Family in the Casino di Pio IV" (fig. 11), observing, "There is an expressive interaction of feelings between the somewhat reserved attitude of the Virgin, the spontaneity of the child's gesture, and St. John's devotion. This kind of composition remained one of Barocci's favourites and is here fully developed for the first time."

37. First published by di Pietro (note 6), pp. 6–8, figs. 7–15.

38. Pillsbury (note 5), pp. 285–87; Ekserdjian (note 7).

39. Pillsbury and Richards (note 2), pp. 39–40, no. 11.

40. Pillsbury and Richards (note 2), p. 39.

41. The strong, recognizable handling of the black chalk hatching is consistent with other black chalk life-sketches of the 1560s, as, for example, in the anatomical details of the *Crucifixion* of 1566. Yet there is rarely, if ever, any crossover between media and intention or scale. Multiple detail studies of figures and limbs do not contain pastel highlights; the large individual studies are generally coloristic and carefully rendered so that they could function as independent works of art.

42. Pillsbury and Richards (note 2), pp. 45–46, no. 18.

43. Ulrich Middeldorf, "Three Italian Drawings in Chicago," *Art in America* 27 (1939), pp. 11–14; see fig. 22.

REED, "Giovanni Benedetto Castiglione's *God Creating Adam*: The First Masterpiece in the Monotype Medium," pp. 66–73.

I am very grateful to Clifford S. Ackley for his assistance, especially for suggesting the relationships between this monotype and sculptural works.

1. The contemporary American artist Michael Mazur, for example, has vividly described his response to a monotype by Edgar Degas in "Monotype: An Artist's View," in New York, The Metropolitan Museum of Art, *The Painterly Print: Monotypes from the Seventeenth to the Twentieth Century*, exh. cat. (New York, 1980), pp. 55–62.

2. The Art Institute purchased the monotype at Christie's, London, Dec. 5, 1985, lot no. 161. The two other monotypes by Castiglione in America are owned by The Metropolitan Museum of Art, New York, and the National Gallery of Art, Washington, D.C.; see *The Painterly Print* (note 1), p. 8 n. 8.

3. See Sue Welsh Reed, "Monotypes in the Seventeenth and Eighteenth Centuries" and entries on Castiglione's monotypes in *The Painterly Print* (note 1), pp. 3–8 and 68–83.

4. Mary Newcome, "A Castiglione-Leone Problem," *Master Drawings* 16, 2 (Summer 1978), p. 168. Newcome also provides biographical data on Castiglione, including his date of birth, first published by P. L. Alfonso, "Gio. Benedetto Castiglione detto il Grechetto," *La berio* 12, 2 (1972), pp. 40–45. The date of the artist's death has only recently been discovered by Ezia Gavazza and Lauro Magnani, and published by Lauro Magnani and Timothy Standring in Genoa, Accademia Ligustica di Belle Arti, *Il genio di Giovanni Benedetto Castiglione: Il Grechetto*, exh. cat. by Gianvittorio Dillon et al. (Genoa, 1990), p. 256.

5. For a thorough discussion of Castiglione as a draftsman, see the Philadelphia Museum of Art, *Giovanni Benedetto Castiglione: Master Draughtsman of the Italian Baroque*, exh. cat. by Ann Percy (Philadelphia, 1971).

6. For a discussion of Castiglione as an etcher, see Boston, Museum of Fine Arts, *Italian Etchers of the Renaissance and Baroque*, exh. cat. by Sue Welsh Reed and Richard Wallace (Boston, 1989), pp. 262–71. All of Castiglione's etchings are reproduced in Paolo Bellini, *The Illustrated Bartsch: Italian Masters of the Seventeenth Century*, vol. 46 (New York, 1985).